Soon Will Come The Light

A View from Inside the Autism Puzzle

By Thomas A. McKean

720 N. Fielder Road
Arlington, TX 76012
800-489-0727
817-277-2270 Fax

http://www.onramp.net/autism - Website
edfuture@onramp.net - email address

Book design & layout by
S.L. Cotton

Third printing 1996.
Includes revisions and additions
to previous printings.

Soon Will Come the Light

Sun goes down, you crawl into bed
feeling all alone.
The dreams you shared throughout the day
were more than yours alone.
But now it's late, duty calls,
and stars form in the skies.
You feel fear as darkness falls
and tears form in your eyes.

You find your bear, hold him tight,
he tries to calm you down.
You hear his soft and gentle words,
though he does not make a sound.
You feel an emptiness inside,
and fears you long to share.
Then you hear voices in the night
you know should not be there.

It's okay, because you are loved,
and that is all you need to know.
Do not fear the darkness,
for soon will come the light.
Stars, they shine, night is warm,
and you will be all right.
Lean back and close your eyes, my child,
sleep peacefully tonight.

Somehow you know he's there with you
and you will be all right.
His love shines through the darkness,
lighting up the room.
The night drifts ever slowly on,
you begin to lose your sight.
When your eyes are finally closed,
you hear him speak to you.

He says, "Come, take my hand.
I'll take you to another land.
Do not fear the darkness,
for soon will come the light.
Stars, they shine, night is warm,
and I know you will be all right.
Lean back and close your eyes, my child,
sleep peacefully tonight.

Relax and dream of lovely things,
sleep peacefully tonight."

Thomas A. McKean

Table of Contents

Acknowledgments

There are several people without whom this book could not have been written. To that end, I would like to thank the following:

My parents, for their continuous and endless financial support.

Wayne Gilpin, for his unprecedented, out-of-the-blue offer to publish this book.

Alex Gilpin, for making his father smile.

Melanie, for the treasured memory of that magical night in the jacuzzi.

Sharon, Mandy, and Laura, for preparing me for Melanie.

Scott Donaldson, for listening intently as I complain about life.

Friend Susanne, wherever I may find her.

Rick Schostek, for his help with the contract.

Jan Serak, for the compassion in her voice, the beauty in her heart, and for introducing me to the White Russian.

Mira Rothenberg, for being the inspiration behind "The Mira Trilogy," which ultimately led to this book.

Neatha Lefevre, because she is my friend.

Veronica Zysk, for her uncanny ability to explain the complex ways of the world to me in words of one syllable.

Bill and Barbara Christopher, who's friendship and tolerance has shown me that even as big as Father Mulcahy's heart is, William Christopher's heart is even bigger.

Temple Grandin, who's ongoing sacrifice, courage, intelligence and talents have not only touched, but also improved the lives of many individuals with autism. Including mine.

Temple Grandin, Sean and Judy Barron, Donna Williams, Annabel Stehli, Charlie Hart and Mira Rothenberg, for showing me how to write a book.

Princess Gwendolyn, for her part in the miracle that brought me out of the shell.

Michael and Gwen Jebb, for believing in me.

The vast membership of the Autism Society of America, who were the long overdue first to wrap their arms around me -- and to give my heart a home.

Dedication

This Book Is Dedicated With Much Love And Affection To Michael and Gwendolyn Jebb.

These are the only people I have ever met in my 28 years that I can say I know, beyond any shadow of a doubt, that they will be my friends forever. All of a sudden, I was no longer alone. Where my world had once been solitary, I now, for the first time, was able to share it with friends.

The details of the friendship and how it led to my eventual, ongoing recovery are touched on in this book. But to use the phrase "touched on" or "tip of the iceberg" or any similar analogy would be to do it an injustice. For it is a much smaller part of a much bigger picture.

For the story to be told correctly, it would take a book far larger than the one you hold in your hands. Perhaps someday, after their two boys have grown a little, the three of us can sit down and write it. I feel this is a project that needs to be done. What we have is a relationship between a person with autism and two people without it. And it is thanks to a lot of work on the part of these two (and maybe just a wee bit of my own doing) that the relationship works. It was their refusing to give up and to search until they found a way to get beyond the autism that led to my recovery. I remember it well. They had a hell of a rough time with it. And I feel that to pass on the knowledge and information of how and why the relationship works can only result in a lot of good for the autistic children in society. All that I have accomplished, both in the autism field and elsewhere, it would not have been possible if I did not have these two to lean on. If they had not found me, my life would have been much different. I honestly believe I would at this moment be locked in one of the institutions until my eventual death. How fortunate I am that it has not happened that way! They are the strength behind the advocacy of Thomas.

The details, if they are ever written, are by necessity at least three or four years into the future. Until then, that book, and even this one, can be accurately and appropriately condensed to the following nine words. Words that I feel for now, and possibly forever, are all that really need to be said:

Thank you, Gwen and Michael. Thanks for loving me.

Preface
A Word from Gwendolyn

I first met Tom in the Fall of 1983. Long haired and scraggly, all I knew was he played the guitar and wore a puzzled expression most of the time. We were both students at a junior college in down state Illinois. He, at 18, having been newly released from the rigors of a mental institution and I, 19, fresh from the halls of a one-year stint at a Bible college.

As time and fate would naturally have it, the threads of our friendship began to interweave and I realized the depths of Tom's "problems" (for that's all I really knew them to be at first; Tom, too, as he had not yet learned of his autism diagnosis). I admit, humbly, to more then once wanting to bow out of the deepening friendship. Could I really handle this? It was my faith, my belief in the claims of Christ that spurred me on at such times.

As I grew and as Tom grew, however, our roles began to be more defined. I began to understand what he wanted in a friend and he began to understand the limits of my friendship. I certainly could not be all things to him. No, what he wanted, what he wants, and really what we all want, is unconditional acceptance: that sweet salve that affirms, reassures, and gives an oh-so-powerful sense that this person loves me, no matter what. With the aid of a mailbox, a phone and annual visits, Tom and I have now spanned over ten years of friendship.

As you read the following pages, I know you will find Tom to be as remarkable as I have. Talented not only in music and in writing, he is a gadgetry wizard. Brave, tender, compassionate, Tom is a work of art in progress. I am privileged to observe the ongoing finishing touches. I love you, Tom.

Gwen Bossingham Jebb
- Winter 1993

Introduction

"I don't want you to go," he said.

"But I have to," I said.

"You have a life to go to," he said, "And I have nothing."

"Yes, you do." You have a life." I said.

"Where?" Tom asked.

"In you," I said. "Look for it inside you." I was not sure that he had the strength in him to do so.

I looked at his beautiful face with those sad, loving, searching eyes, trying desperately to get into mine. And that smile. That strange smile that was no smile at all, but a grimace. The demand in that being was too strong to bear. His sadness was too heavy. His need too great, so I sent him on his way.

I was at the airport in Columbus, Ohio, heading back home to New York. Tom McKean was autistic.

Much of my life I have worked with autistic children. I have loved them and tried to understand them, but they were always children. Only children. Tom McKean was grown up. Twenty-six-years old, grown up.

In the summer of 1991, I got a telephone call. The conversation went like this.

" I am Tom McKean. I have read your book. I liked it very much. How do you know so much about autism? Are you autistic?" He spoke in a monotone. His speech was exact, stilted.

"Wait a minute," I interrupted. "How did you get my telephone number? It is unlisted."

He laughed and said, "I am very ingenious. It was very clever of me, but I got it. I am a twenty-six-year-old autistic man."

xi

My ears perked up. My antennae went up. Now his manner of speech made sense.

"I write well, too. Poetry. Stories. Compose music and invent." I love your book and wanted to say 'hi' to you and do something for you."

"You write!" I exclaimed. "Write to me about yourself. Write what it is like to be autistic. Write me your story. What it feels like to be you. Your feelings, your thoughts. What you can do. What you cannot do. And why. What you need to be happy. What makes you unhappy. How you are different from people who are not autistic. Write, write, write!" I went on like a lunatic.

After the phone call I wondered, is it true? Is he for real? Is he putting me on? A real, live, autistic adult who can talk and make sense? And tells me directly what it feels like to be autistic? Will these be his thoughts? His experiences? At last, will I be able to hear what it is like to be autistic from someone who is autistic-instead of having to imagine it?

A thousand times I had tried to imagine. A thousand times I had to guess, had to use my intuition in order to know the child who was in my care. Never once could the child tell me what it felt like to be autistic. He could only give me clues.

Tom McKean, the autistic child who had grown into a man, at long last was going to tell me his story, without my having to imagine everything.

In August of 1991, I received a two-hundred-page letter which, after many revisions, became this book.

I was not sure that Tom existed. I had to find out. I went to Ohio. Many of my friends tried to dissuade me. "How do you know he's not an axe murderer?" they said. When I got off the plane, I saw a man standing by a column. He looked curled up upon himself, as if he was trying to disappear. I walked straight to him, gave him my knapsack, and with a "Hi, Tom," went straight to his home. He was autistic.

His home was full of machinery. Videos, radios, computers, telephones, various communication systems, clocks and a hearing apparatus attached to his phone. All had been invented by Tom. Strange labyrinths of a different world.

I spent three days in Ohio. All that time, Tom held on to my hand with such strength that I had to remind him not to break it. Tom had to "connect" with me. He had no choice. He had to stare into my eyes with such intensity that separation became impossible.

All along, we talked. And he told and told, and we talked. I met his family.

For over thirty years, I have been interested in, and worked with, autistic children. I have set up centers for them, fought for them, written about them. My ideas of what made them tick changed with time. My ideas about the causes of autism changed with time. That the children existed, loved, felt, thought, ached, raged, felt happiness, never changed. And that they had a right to happiness, and they could be helped, like the rest of us, never left me. They are a part of the human race.

We are not autistic. The autistic are not us. The autistic child follows a different drummer. He is the different drummer. To understand him and help him, we must follow him. Some of them accomplish feats that none of us can. Many are much smarter than we are, and many are less capable.

When the autistic children did not seem to understand, I felt that they could. When they did not seem to hear, I knew they did. When they did not speak in words, they "spoke" in a different way. It was we who did not understand their language. The inadequacy was ours, not theirs. We were on a different wavelength. We had no right to ignore them just because we did not understand them. Too often we do not comprehend their gifts.

They live in a strange, internal world. The yardstick by which we measure our world does not necessarily fit theirs.

They walk in a maze, understandable only to them, recognizable only by them. We do not possess enough imagination or intuitive knowledge or freedom to talk to them. We fail them, and they walk alone through life. Tom McKean is an autistic child who grew into an autistic man, who walks through the maze and can lead us through it with him. He walks alone, but he also has friends.

xiii

Tom McKean wrote me his letter, two hundred pages of it, and told me many things about the autistic person. Some things I knew over thirty years ago, for which I could not find words, things I dared not express; And many, many things I never knew. The autistic child/man said to me in words that I had wordlessly felt, and he corroborated what I thought I knew and believed.

This year is the beginning of 1994. I've kept a contact with and maintained a friendship with Tom these past three years. I watched him grow and develop. I saw the metamorphosis of an autistic human being. It was like watching a painting emerge from the artist's brush, the canvas becoming more and more complete. So it is watching Tom McKean grow. He is both the painter and the work of art.

After Tom's "letter" to me, word got around about what he had written. More and more people read it. He started to be invited to meetings of parents with autistic children. He began to explain their children's actions to them. He spoke of the children's needs, and he emphasized that each child is an individual. He became more and more known in the field of autism. He began to travel from city to city, and to make more speeches. He wrote more and more poetry, and he wrote additions to his "letter" to me. He was elected to the board of directors of the Autism Society of America. He organized a group of adult autistic people so they would not feel isolated.

Last summer, I saw Tom at the International Conference on Autism. He was no longer the shy, curled, inward, withdrawn, and lonely human being I saw in Ohio in 1991. He stood straighter; his head higher. His face was alive with feeling. His hands no longer tried to clutch mine, nor did his eyes bore into everyone's eyes. He delivered his speech and proceeded to play the guitar and sing a song which he had composed. Remarkable!

This book allows us to see where before we were blind. Anybody; you, me, teacher, therapist, mother, father, psychiatrist, psychologist, can learn from this book, and our learning will help us to help the autistic.

Mira Rothenberg
Author - *Children with Emerald Eyes*

xiv

Foreword

I am still in awe of the way it happened. One night, I am just another of the many people with autism in the United States. Living on welfare and going nowhere fast. I am, by necessity, content with the private little projects I do for my own amusement. I have no job, no future, no real grip on reality. I have no female companion and I do not want one. On the outside, I try to look happy. Inside, I am dying. I hunger for more. To make a difference in the world. To leave a positive impression. I want to contribute and I am unable to. And this makes me profoundly sad. I smile in the company of others, I cry in the darkness when I am alone, clutching my bear tight. Perhaps, at that moment, the only friend I have.

And then the next night I blink my eyes. And there was nothing different. Not that could be easily seen, anyway. My eyes close and I am nobody. When they open again, I am an international role model.

My mailbox begins to fill with letters from people all over the country. And then from all over the world. "Thank you for being there," they say. "You have no idea how much help you have been to me." Others ask questions that are so easily answered. It interests me (and it still does) that they are unable to find those answers on their own.

Intermixed with that mail is the regularly appearing plane ticket. Again and again I pack my suitcase, bear and computer, and go talk to people who quickly become my friends. And then I smile when someone gives me a check for something that has been nothing but fun for me the whole time.

Four times a year I attend a national board meeting of the Autism Society of America. Sometimes my views are met with controversy in the board room. But I have gotten used to this. I have learned to understand that I am the only one in that room who has been there. The rest have only been able to observe it from the sidelines. Some of them understand me, some do not. Some try and are unable to, some do not even bother to try at all. I feel a sense of power and an even bigger sense of responsibility when I take that seat. And sometimes it is overwhelming to me. I hear from many people that they wish it was them who was sitting there. One person, I've never met, goes so far as to threaten my life and the lives of my friends. The FBI nails him and I realize how honored I am to have the position I do.

I come to realize that no matter how long ago I have done something, that something will not be forgotten. With one debatable exception, I was the first person with a disability to nationally publish the personal results of auditory training (see Part Two). Over a year later, I still receive mail about it. Where I want the phone modification and pressure bracelets I designed to remain in my past, they both still come up frequently. As does the song I did at the Toronto Conference. These are just a few examples.

When I started writing this, the first thing I did was just make a few minor changes to the *Mira Trilogy* (a collection of letters I wrote to Mira Rothenberg). Then, I realized that what I wrote in it was mainly guess work. Yes, most of it was an accurate guess, but it was still just a guess. Since I have written it, I have evolved and gained knowledge. I felt it would be a crime to not put that knowledge in.

As I was rewriting it, I came to realize that unlike the *Mira Trilogy*, this was going to be published. And as such it was subject to reviews. I wanted to please everybody. I knew it was impossible. But I tried anyway. Nothing got done and I felt a heavy burden of stress. The deadline grew near. I needed a new approach. I called several people to ask for advice and then decided that the only way this project was going to have any merit at all was if I printed only what I believe to be the truth.

What I *think* is the truth, what I have reason to *believe* is the truth, what I *know* is the truth, and/or what I am willing to *defend* as the truth, that is what you will find in the following pages. Nothing else. There are no embellishments here. My life does not need any. If this is to be remembered like the other things I have done, let it be remembered as the truth.

They say (and we have all heard too many times) that when life hands you lemons, you make lemonade. This seemed impossible for me. Then I made one phone call to one person I had never met, and that set off a domino effect that would change my life forever. I was not entirely grounded in reality when I called Mira (as you read in her introduction). Had I known what the end result of that call was going to be, I never would have called her. I would have been too frightened.

Or perhaps it began even before that. We have also heard too many times that things happen when you least expect it. And when I least expected it,

I found a prospective wife. Then when I least expected it, I lost her. But had I not lost her, I never would have started searching for the truth of Thomas. And so none of this would have ever happened.

Yes, I am only one person. Yes, this is only one biography out of many. But perhaps if there is an answer, an answer to war, to hunger, to the end of famine and disease, to all that plagues mankind, it lies here in what you are now doing. In the effort of each individual to understand his fellow man, one person at a time.

Thomas A. McKean

Parents, please be careful in the way you raise your children. You never know when one of them may grow up to write a book about you.

Part I

My Life with Autism

"I am tired of denying who I am. I will no longer do this. To myself or to the people I love. But before I can know, love, and accept who I am, and who I am growing into, I must find that person inside of me."

-Thomas A. McKean

CHAPTER ONE

I Leave my Home for a "Home"

It was a warm, summer day in central Ohio. Friends were in the back yard playing and awaiting the festivities. Mother was in the kitchen cooking brownies. I was in there with her.

She took the brownies out of the oven. Together, we walked outside. Friends gathered around the picnic table in anticipation. I sat down and suddenly felt a wave of terror unlike any I had ever felt before.

This was my fifth birthday party, and the first inkling I had that something was desperately wrong.

For several years after that, the presence of other people around me would be terrifying. And the more people there were, the more terrifying it would be.

I am the third of four children born to financially comfortable parents. My father worked for 30 plus years at Nationwide Insurance, writing policies for them before retiring to start an antique business. My mother is an English major with a Masters Degree in Early Childhood Education. The latter confuses me somewhat. It seems to me that anyone who has a masters degree in such an area would know what autism is. By its very definition, it must be evident in childhood. Usually within the first 36 months. Add to that the fact that she herself suspected autism even before I was two years old (1967). (However, in fairness, her suspicion was not confirmed or in any way reinforced by any doctor.) Still, I fail to see why there was a strong lack of emotional support as I was growing up.

But that support was not there. Or perhaps it was, but I certainly do not remember it. I was yelled at and punished quite a bit for what I did (and for what I did not do). Everything that happened, it was entirely my own fault. There was no one (or nothing) else that it could be blamed on. But my recent intense research has shown me that I was doing exactly what a young autistic child was supposed to be doing. I was making my parents life a living hell. (And, I must add, I was quite good at it.) I feel now that I was performing as I was expected to, perhaps even going above and beyond the call of duty in the name of dedication to my job. Why did they not see this? Maybe I was doing my job too well?

As you may suspect, school was a nightmare. I attended kindergarten at Valley Forge Elementary School here in Columbus. I stayed there until the third grade. That is when everything went south on me.

Somehow the powers-that-be in the Columbus Public School system decided that I was to be placed in the Learning Disabled classes. This proved to be a very bad move. Because every half year or year, I was transferred to a different school. I feel that no child, especially an autistic one, should have to be submitted to the horrors that go along with that. And if this autism proves hereditary, and I should someday have an autistic child, I will not let that happen! My parents and others were always asking why I didn't have any friends. Perhaps one answer was because they never let me stay in one place long enough to make any!

It was here in the LD classes that I learned one of the most important things I have ever learned about humanity. Humanity has a nagging habit of criticizing that which it does not understand. There are precious few people who are not autistic that understand autism. It was also during this time the doctors gave me an artificial eardrum in my right ear. I was scheduled to be in the hospital for three days, but I was there for a week because I had no balance. When it was time to leave, they couldn't find a wheelchair so I was wheeled to the car in a little red wagon.

Sixth grade came around, and I was to discover that I had come full circle. I was once again at Valley Forge. It was here that I started writing. Just a little. Nobody really liked what I wrote. I have since come to see that writing may be a natural ability for some people, but it is like any other talent in that it must be developed. I have been writing regularly now for 11 years. I think I have the hang of it. During this time, one of my brothers left home. This was 1978/1979. He has not been seen since.

Seventh grade marked the end of my education for a long time. I never finished. Throughout the course of my life, for as long as I can remember, I had seen one doctor right after the other. Each one shaking their head in puzzlement over what may have been wrong with me. "We're sorry, Mrs. McKean. We know something is wrong, but we don't know what it is." Finally, at age 14, I received the diagnosis. At this point. the solution was simple. I would "be admitted to a psychiatric institution for a period of three weeks." Well, she was half right. It was three years. One day, my mother put me on her lap in the living room. (This may well have been the last time that ever happened. And I will always remember it well.) I was around 12 or 13 at the time. She told me I

4

was "going away" for a while, and that this was good because I did not have to take finals at school.

What a deal! How could I refuse? No finals? It was a junior high school student's dream come true! Meanwhile, I had throughout the years continued to realize that there was something seriously wrong somewhere. I think any child who goes through the social interaction that I did would realize this. So I began to search for answers as to what that something might be. But no one bothered to tell me I was autistic, so I never found it.

I was admitted into the hospital on June 3, 1980. Just 15 days before my fifteenth birthday. My grandfather brought me a chess set for my birthday that year. It is unfortunate that he died shortly thereafter. Up to that time, he was one of the very few people in my life that I had any respect for. (He was a retired Presbyterian minister.) I now remember talking to him in the middle of the night, wondering if maybe he could hear me. To this day, that chess set is one of my most treasured possessions.

The first thing I remember about my institutional period are my thoughts as I walked out the front door of my home with my bear tucked under my arm. It was around 10:00 a.m. My parents were already outside, walking toward the car. As I stepped out on to the porch, my thoughts were on the Hobbit. Bilbo was correct, I thought, in that "the greatest adventure is what lies ahead."

The only entrance to the hospital is over a bridge. As we crossed the bridge for the first time, I pondered if maybe the main reason they built that bridge there was for the symbolism. And in my case, it worked. It made me wonder if I was crossing the barrier into a "Fantasy Land," a term I would later use many times to describe it as that place was as close to an alternate dimension as you can possibly come.

Our first stop was the administration building. All I remember about this is being bored for about an hour while some guy in a suit talked to my parents, and being rather perturbed that my parents basically did nothing but tell him how bad I was.

Then we went to basement of the young adolescent unit. This is where I would be living for the next two years. More talk. And I met the doctor. I was not too impressed with him at first, which is why I never really did open up to him all that much. Eventually, we followed him (or someone) down a hall, who opened the door to the stairwell. We climbed the stairs, and I stepped into my new home.

All I saw at first was a big room with a small kitchen behind it. There was tile on the floor and a lot of tables which had the kind of chairs around them that made your legs look like waffles. There was only one child in the whole room and he was working on building a model ship. I later found out his name was Scott. We were never really close. In fact, when I accidentally ran into him years later at a Pizza Hut, he gave me his number but I never called him.

Walking in a little more, I was able to see a fairly good sized recreation room with a nice pool table, stereo, and a lot of comfortable chairs and couches. Every last wall was kind of an off-white color, but this was compensated for by the green carpeting. It looked a bit like grass. Off the side of the rec room was a tiny room with a lot of windows. This turned out to be the designated smoking area. I never went in.

To the right, left, and front of the dining room were three other areas, which I later discovered were called "pods." They were all color coded. To the left was the yellow pod, the front had the red pod, and to the right was the blue pod. Each pod was again separated, this time into bedrooms. Each pod had five bedrooms; three double rooms and two single rooms. The colors of the pods indicated who would be sleeping there. The yellow was for the girls, the blue was for the boys, leaving the red pod to be the most coveted co-ed pod. I was fortunate enough to spend most of my nights in the red pod.

Each pod had two bathrooms. Each bathroom had a shower, a sink, and a standard separate stall for the toilet. I think the reason for this was because there were some people who were not allowed to "go" without staff supervision (no, I was not one of them, thankfully). So by using the stall, the patient still had some privacy.

I found there were many advantages to living in the co-ed pod. For while it is true that they did not pair any males and females together, that did not stop us from sneaking into each other's rooms in the middle of the night. What others did, that you will have to ask them. I was usually only looking for a hug, which I always found. I would then gladly sneak back to my own room and go to bed. It also came in handy with the letter passing, one of the very few effective forms of therapy. The staff did not like the way we all passed little written words of support back and forth, so we had to find some way of doing it without them noticing. One of the ways I found was to sneak into the girls bathroom and leave it there. The staff had their own, so they rarely, if ever, went in. This usually worked out well. Whoever found the note would pass it along. Occasionally though, one of the girls would walk in on me. But really this was not even a problem.

6

If you ever end up in an institution, for whatever reason, you may discover that in some cases, modesty is best left alone. Eventually you realize this, and you quit trying altogether. The laws of nature that existed in this domain were completely different than what we are used to now. And one of those laws was, in some ways, a concept of "unisex" among the patients. We were all one. At times it was the other way around. A girl would be in the guys room, and a guy would walk in. It is ironic that you had to be (relatively) healthy for this to work. Those who were a little more "off the deep end" were confined to the torture of the single sex pods. During the entire time I was there, I probably did around six months in the male pod, and that was spread out over a period of two years. I was always happy to get back to the co-ed pod. There was a real feeling of love and family in that pod that did not exist in the other two.

Behind the yellow (girls) pod, between the pod and the smoking area, were three other areas. The first was the TV room. This is where you went when you were in the mood for a good argument. There was always someone who wanted to watch a different show. Alternately, if everyone was in a good mood, you could sit on the couch and watch TV while you snuggled that cute person sitting next to you. At least until the staff caught you.

Behind that was what they called the "Meds Closet." This is where you went to get your daily dose of Thorazine, vitamins, or whatever. I was told to take a vitamin and a couple cans of Ensure Plus every day. If I did not want to, they did on a couple occasions threaten to put me into solitary, strap me down, and force feed me.

Off to the side of the closet was the solitary confinement area. This consisted of two rooms called, "Special Care." But I am not sure that is an accurate title or description. I observed that those who were put in there were usually put in there at the times when they most needed love and support. Such things are hard to come by when you are all alone. Seemed the only thing you could do was sit there with your legs crossed and watch your wrists bleed some more. I am no doctor, but I fail to see any therapeutic value in this.

The clothes were very different. The staff worried (possibly rightfully so) that the potentially suicidal patients would somehow try to use their clothes to hang themselves. So special clothes were designed to make this an impossibility. And while they did what they were supposed to do, they were not exactly what you might call high fashion.

Fundamental human needs were sometimes ignored or exploited. The staff were required, after putting you in here, to check in on you every fifteen minutes. You were not allowed any human contact whatsoever. Now, you have to understand that this room is just what the word "room" implies. It was a floor, a ceiling, and four walls. There was a small mattress (also specially designed, and very uncomfortable), but that was it. Up close to the ceiling, there was a very, very small window. Just beneath the window was the door to the bathroom, which was required to remain locked. The good part of this was that with a little balance, you could climb up on the doorknob and look out the window. But they made it just as difficult as they possibly could.

Staff would usually just peer in through a very small window in the door, and leave. Occasionally, about once every hour, one would come in and ask if you had to go to the bathroom. Most answered no to this, even when they were pretty desperate. Another requirement was that the staff member stay with you while you go. The rules (obviously) state that the staff must be of the same sex, but sometimes they weren't. And sometimes, there was just nothing the patient could do about it but accept it. Once in a rare while, someone with a just a bit of real compassion would come along. You had to jump at the opportunity. They broke the rules for you, actually treated you like a real person. They would not only sit in there and talk to you (and hold you, and let you cry), but they would also unlock the bathroom door, and let you close it and take your time. This also went for the specially designed shower that was installed in there. Bizarre looking thing, but totally "safe." You may think that closing a bathroom door is no big deal, but such things were not an absolute in solitary, and you counted your blessings when it happened.

Personally, I was only in there once. But I was only in there for six hours, so there was no real problem. There were some who spent days, weeks, even months under the above conditions. (Just as a side note, I observed throughout my stay that the females spent much more time in there than the males did.)

Finally, across from the kitchen was the staff office. This was basically where the staff worked when they weren't working anywhere else. This is where all your records and charts were kept, and where you were not allowed to go, under any circumstances.

There was a desk in front of the office. This is where the unit secretary worked. She would answer calls and hand out your mail. Sometimes staff looked through the mail first. Thankfully, this was rare, I think.

Whoever had the job of sitting at that desk all day had to be a very special person. And they took great care in picking the right person for the job. They knew you would talk to her when you did not want to talk to the regular staff. Unfortunately, all they could do was listen. But the two who had the position while I was there both had an uncanny ability to listen. They probably kept me from going completely crazy more than once.

I was led around the corner, past the desk, into the blue (male) pod. I believe it was room 11. (Rooms were numbered 1 through 15.) A nurse came in with a clipboard and spent a few hours asking me questions (which I rarely answered honestly) and taking blood tests. It was very annoying. I guess after that, I really had no choice but to settle down and get used to the place. The nurse and I later went on to become good friends.

One of the first things I learned is that freedom was a variable. Another bent rule of nature, most of us define freedom as black or white. You either have it or you don't. Such was not the case here. There was an elaborate set of red tape in this area.

Freedom came in different levels. In fact, when referencing these levels, that is what they were called. "Levels." The first, and lowest, was "Regular." But there was nothing regular about it at all. It basically meant you were a prisoner. You could go to the "therapeutic activities" that were assigned to you on grounds, but that is it. Other than that, you were confined to the unit.

The next rung on the levels ladder was "A.A.C." This stood for "Accompanied to Activities in the Community." With this status, you could once in a while go off grounds for some activity in the community. I found this to be not so much to my liking. Because among other things, this meant that they came in and woke you up at the crack of dawn on the weekend, and you went on a hiking trip in one of the fine metropolitan parks here in Columbus. I would rather sleep. So was not that you had the option of going out, you were forced to go out.

Occasionally, you would get to go to a movie. This was always nice. Sometimes you could walk to the local mall. This was not nice. you could look at all the merchandise, but you were, as a rule, unable to buy anything due to limited funds. If you wanted to stay in bed during the morning, they would not let you. I once had a staff member come in the room and literally tip the bed over top of me to wake me up.

Next was "U.A." which meant "Unaccompanied to Activities." Here we finally get into some freedom. The activities referred to here are the activities on grounds. These were usually meant as a way to vent your anger and frustration about being there or about whatever else you had to be angry about.

While it was very easy to abuse this privilege, few of us who had it did. Usually the people who ran away were those on one of the previous two levels. You need to admire the creativity with which they came up with these schemes to get out, because most (if not all) of them worked. The only problem is that soon they would get hungry. Then what?

Next to last was "Grounds." That meant on a sunny day, you could take a walk with that cute girl in the pod. They just opened the door and let you out. This was abused constantly. There is a ravine on the border of the hospital, and ravines and institutionalized teenagers are not a good combination. I'm sure you can see where this is going...

Finally, "Towns." The ultimate freedom (such as it was). You were free to leave the hospital at any time. So long as you came back before dark. That is the long and the short of it. I actually did get this high, but I never used it. There was never any reason for me to leave the hospital. It was like a city for the insane. Everything you needed was there. Hospital, stores, food, medical supplies, everything. We were a world in and of ourselves. The surrounding community liked this fact. It meant that they did not have to deal with us.

So how was it determined which one of these freedoms was allotted to you at any particular moment? Every Tuesday there were what they called "team meetings." Each person was assigned a doctor when they came in. Each doctor is assigned a "team." A team is a select group of the nurses, psych-techs and a teacher who work with that particular patient on a more elaborate effort than what the rest of the staff do. Which team you were assigned to when you are admitted seemed to depend mainly on who had room for an extra person.

So each Tuesday, those who were assigned to any particular doctor would get together with the staff team. (My meetings were usually in the TV room.) You would go around the room, one by one, and the other patients on that team would tell the staff whether you deserve a promotion or not, based on your general conduct during the previous week. In other words, you were tried by a jury of your peers. The team then met on Thursdays to give an overview of each patient assigned to the doctor. Occasionally, someone on the team would say, "He has done well," and you would be granted the next highest level.

It also went the opposite way; if you did something the staff did not like (which I was well-known for doing), they had the authority, much used, to bust you down to whatever they felt was appropriate. It was somewhat like a court martial.

10

It should be noted here that standard policy dictated that the third shift look in on you once every hour. There were usually only two staff members on night shift. One was a female nurse, the other a male psych-tech. And depending on who you were, and who did the checks on any particular hour, it had a profound impact on you the rest of the night. If you were female, and the psych-tech looked in on you, he would sometimes check you over a little too "closely." Fortunately this did not happen often, but it did happen. Conversely, if you were male, and the nurse did the rounds, the worst thing that could possibly happen was for you to hold out your arms and have her come give you a big hug and a light kiss on the cheek, followed by a soft "Good Night" whispered in your ear.

Policy also said that once you went in for the night, you were under absolutely no circumstances to come out of your room until after midnight. And even then, you had better have a very good reason. Occasionally this would be a problem, but it usually wasn't. Other than the routine hourly checks, the staff basically sat around and did their own thing, leaving us free to do whatever we wanted. And we usually did. We couldn't go out into the main room or anything, but we could easily sneak back and forth between any room in our own particular pod. Sometimes the staff would catch us. Usually they didn't.

Just next to my unit, and connected by the underground tunnel where the doctors offices were, was another unit. This is where all of the older adolescents stayed. While I was there, they built the school on grounds just next to the adolescent complex. The school up until then was in an old trailer. The new school was nice! It had big classrooms with a lot of windows that you could look out of if you did not feel like working. Eventually, the school adopted a couple of Chinchillas and kept them in the teachers lounge. Between the school and adolescent wing, they built a nice little paved area where you could play volleyball, basketball, or some such game. The trailer that used to be the school was remodeled, and now serves as an office for a few of the social workers.

There were also many other buildings. One was the campus center. This is where all of the adjunctive therapists worked. There was also a "campus store." Each patient was allotted six dollars spending cash per week, for use over in the campus store. It was the general store type of place, carrying your basic necessities, plus stationary, candy, and a few inspirational books for anyone who wanted to buy them. Eventually they added a rather large display of stuffed animals. The price on all items was marked down to wholesale for benefit of the patients. But sometimes, depending on who was working there on any particular day, you could get things even cheaper. Some of the best prices in all of Ohio can be found in the campus store, and I have gone back there many times for specific items.

Across from the campus store was the chapel. Too small for anyone to get married in, but to the best of my knowledge, no one has ever wanted to get married there anyway. Still, it had a nice organ and the hospital chaplain did a vespers service there every week. Very few attended. One interesting thing about religion is that the founders of the hospital were Seventh Day Adventists, and they pushed those beliefs on us constantly. The laundry room was locked from sundown Friday until sundown Saturday every week, and there was no meat allowed for breakfast or lunch. Instead, they had us eat a vegetable protein mix from soybeans that was supposed to taste like meat, but of course it never did.

The basement of the campus center held the main gym. Beautiful piece of work. They spared no expense. Off to the side of the gym was another little room with a pool table, and a few ping-pong tables.

There were other units on grounds. Where you were assigned depended on your age and what your diagnosis was.

Up in the top floor of the emergency services unit was where the campus paper was printed. That is also where "Windows and Mirrors" was made, a rather unique monthly poetry magazine. The campus paper was a weekly newsletter called "The Analyst." I wrote a few articles and designed a few covers for it while I was there. (This experience would later help me when I would write articles for A.S.A.'s publication, *The Advocate*.)

The basement of one of the units had a music room. Pianos, drums, guitars, banjos, just about every musical instrument you could think of. This is also where the monthly "coffeehouses" were held. Those with musical talent (and those without) would get up on stage and sing their hearts out.

There was a horticultural/activity center just beyond the bridge. We used to plant strawberries there every year. And there was a cafeteria just next to the campus center. The food made without the use of the vegetable protein always tasted better than the other, but it was very hard to come by.

An outpatient facility was built on grounds. It was called "A.D.T.," which stood for "Adolescent Day Treatment." (They abbreviated everything.) I spent my last year there in that facility.

Six months after I was admitted, I began writing again. This may be one of the best things that ever happened to me, but it happened quite by accident. One of the girls had recently tried the standard wrist-slashing routine and was in solitary. I decided it would maybe be nice to come up with some clever way to tell her that I love her and that I was thinking about her. So I got a card and I

12

wrote her a little note. I had to choose my nurse carefully. I knew that most, if not all of them would follow policy and not allow Heidi to have it. But the only way I could get it to her was through a nurse. I chose my nurse, still thinking that it was a hopeless endeavor. I was wrong. The nurse went into solitary and gave Heidi my card. When Heidi finally got out, the first thing she did was to give me a big hug and thank me and tell me how special it was to her. That was the first time in my life that a hug felt like what it was supposed to. I became instantly addicted to the feeling, which was to cause problems later on (and it still does). I also became addicted to writing. I concluded that if it had helped her that much, maybe I was actually good at it.

I was also taking guitar lessons. My abilities in this area soon surpassed the abilities of the instructor. (I had no idea at the time that I had savant music abilities.) Naturally, I put these two things together and began writing songs. I have since gone on to do some studio work, recording just a few (33) of those songs I wrote in there and the songs I wrote after I got out. One song, "Dreamchild," went on to win an award. It is sad to note that I am neither writing songs nor doing the studio work anymore. Recording in the studio, while always a thrill, is not the thrill that it once was. You will find the lyrics to Dreamchild (and many more of the 33 songs) in the back of this book.

Things were different in the hospital. There was no one to yell at me, and so the rest of the autism, which up to that point I had somehow buried without dealing with, began to surface. I would occasionally retreat from the world into my own reality. It took me many years to figure this out, but I believe I have found a way to leave the gateway between realities unlocked in such a way that I can bounce back and forth very easily. I feel that if people with autism can master this skill, they have a superior advantage over the general population. (This world too stressful? Hey, I'm outta here!) Speech became a problem. My L's became Y's. My D's became G's. My speech would just hang and stutter. My hands were forever shaking (sometimes along with the rest of me). I have heard rumors from many people that when I pass into my own world, whatever that world may be, my eyes go from brown to a very light gray. One cannot see their own eyes, so I have no way to validate this. I am not so sure I believe it, but a lot of people have noted it and I would be interested in knowing someday. Some people who are supposedly "in the know" on these things say it is very possible. Others say that the eyes simply can't change colors. The limited psionic sensors (such as they are) also made their first appearance around this time, and I will go into detail about that later.

It is true that time has a way of distorting memories, yet there are things and events about my hospital stay I shall always remember. Some I will remember fondly. Most I wish I could forget. Here are some examples.

13

* * *

As mentioned, one therapy they used was music therapy. I was in a band called, "Us." (Come listen to Us, etc. etc.) We put a few songs together and then the proud (and talented?) teenagers invited parents and friends to the hospital for the concert. It was a smashing success, and the first time I was ever asked to sign an autograph.

The nurse who directed the band took us all out for pizza down the street to celebrate. We were happy. Looking back, the night had not been spectacular, yet those of us with a natural drive or need to make quality music had done so. And we were proud.

It was dark by the time we got back to the hospital. We were smiling and laughing and telling stories as we parked the van around back and walked into the back door. Our self esteem was up, which was a rare occurrence, and it seemed like we had been given a treasured memory that night. It seemed as though there was nothing that could possibly ruin that night, or take that memory away from us.

We walked in the door only to step into a thick trail of blood.

The magic of the moment rapidly disappeared, and would be gone forever. We walked in the rest of the way cautiously and silently. None of us knew who it was, but we all instinctively knew what it was.

My eyes were on the floor, following the trail. I knew where it would lead before I followed it, yet I felt compelled to follow it anyway. Slowly, I became aware of someone crying. It was a crying like someone in pain. I looked up to see her. The nurse had her arm wrapped around her, and she was leading her slowly into solitary. I watched silently, with the others, the blood falling heavily from her wrists to the floor as she was led around the corner and out of sight.

What had caused her to do this? Did she truly want to die or was she crying for help? Would they find a way to help her? Did she just want attention? Why was she so desperate then that she went as far as she did? These questions and others pervaded my thoughts that night. The cuts were deep and required stitches, but she survived.

Months later, I would find the answers to those questions when I also tried to end my own life.

14

CHAPTER TWO

"Interesting" Associations in the "Home"

As I also mentioned, the only way into the hospital was over the bridge. And usually, to cross that bridge without prior permission was grounds for punishment. Below the bridge, *far* below, was a ravine and the small brook that ran under the bridge. I was standing one day on the bridge, looking down and pondering the questions any adolescent in an institution would ponder when I was joined by a fellow patient living in another building.

I did not know him that well other than that I had seen him and talked to him a few times. He engaged me in conversation about various popular topics. How cute the girls were, how ugly the food was. I continued to look over the bridge to the brook below.

I blinked my eyes and found myself suspended over the bridge. I am still not exactly sure how it happened. I looked up and saw this man holding me over the bridge with an evil smile on his face. I made the mistake of looking down and I realized that if he dropped me, it was the end of Thomas. I also realized that he had every intention of dropping me.

I pulled myself up frantically and wrapped my arms tightly around his neck, trying to position myself in such a way that if I went down, at least he would go down with me. He continued to hold me and my life in his hands, laughing at the thought that he had the power to kill me, which indeed he did have at that moment. I was terrified. I had no idea what to do or how to get out of this. Or even if I *would* get out of this.

He held me there for what seemed like forever. And the more time went by, the more certain I was that I was going to die. Then I blinked my eyes again and I was back on the bridge. He apologized and walked away calmly, as if nothing had happened. I fell to my knees, closed my eyes, and my breathing slowly returned to normal.

One unwritten policy that the various patients abide by is to protect each other. And I can certainly see the need to do this. I had previously seen policy broken many times and did nothing about it. And God knows I did my own share of breaking policy more than once. The reason I did it, the reason they *all* did it, was simply related to survival. And nobody understood that more

15

than I did. But I made an exception in this case and told the staff about this incident. I did not see how protecting him would help him. And I did not want to be the silent accessory to the next person he did that to, especially if he decided to let go.

There was an investigation. He was found guilty and released from the hospital, back into society. I guess they decided that was where he belonged.

The bridge has since been remodeled. It is no longer possible to put a person's life in danger by holding them over the bridge.

* * *

One of my personal favorite hobbies while I was there was to sneak into the cafeteria and scarf some chocolate chip cookies. After many months of staking out the cafeteria, I had created a system by which I could get in and take them and get out undetected. Those cookies were one of the very rare tolerable foods that they served.

I was walking along the grounds of the hospital one day, casually eating some freshly stolen cookies. I was joined by Gar, a friend of mine in one of the adult units. I gave him a cookie and we stared talking.

Eventually we found ourselves deep in the ravine by the train tracks. This was forbidden territory, and I wonder to this day how I got there. Gar all of a sudden pulled all of his pants down and put his arms around me.

I very gently, as kindly and compassionately as I could, took Gar's arms off of me and put them back down by his side. Gar looked at me confused and dumbfounded.

"Tom?"

"Yes?"

"Well, [pause] I thought... I thought... Nothing. Never mind."

Gar turned to relieve himself on the tree. He pulled himself together and walked away. A week later, I ran into Gar again as I was casually eating stolen cookies. He was glad to see me as it gave him a chance to apologize. I believe his apology was genuine. Should I run into Gar again, I will consider him a friend.

Several months after this incident occurred, I went into the cafeteria to steal some cookies. I had been doing this for some time now, and this time it was very easy. There was a bowl of them set out on the cookie shelf and no one was around. It was like these cookies were screaming at me to take them, so I did.

I took them back to my room where myself and my roommate ate them happily. Later that night, my roommate ran into the bathroom and vomited. Half an hour or so later, I got up to run into the bathroom to vomit, but I didn't make it in time. It was more violent than it had ever been before, and has ever been since.

Suffice it to say I got the message. That was the last day I stole cookies from the cafeteria.

* * *

The way the graveyard shift worked was that we were all assigned to go to bed around 10:00 p.m. There were two people on duty. A female nurse and a male psychiatric technician. One of these guys later proved to be a little too enthusiastic about his job.

Yes, we enjoyed aggravating the midnight staff once in a while. None of us wanted to be there. So one night I came up with a device designed specifically for this purpose.

The device consisted of a small, plastic chalice type of bowl, some string, and a few other items. What it amounted to when it was finished was a technical version of the classic bucket of water over the door. The idea was for the nurse to come in, get far enough in that she felt nothing would happen, and get her at that point. My roommate and I worked for about an hour setting it up just so.

It worked perfectly. She walked in and I drenched her. What I did not know is that this particular evening, she was wearing a rather expensive silk dress. And the dress was pretty much ruined that night.

In order to keep this from happening again, I modified the device so poker chips would fall instead of water.

The device was confiscated for a period of time, after which it was given back to me. I laid low for a while and then we set it up again when they least expected it. We rigged it for poker chips and again we were successful. This

17

time the nurse we got was Madeline. And to celebrate our second victory, I named the device the "Madeline Machine." I modified the device for portability and we began to covertly pass the Madeline Machine around to various rooms so they would never know which room was rigged. From that time on, all nurses and technicians would open the door to every room and stand back for a moment. The Madeline Machine soon became obsolete. But not before many successes. And the influence it left behind would be felt, even years later.

What we were unaware of is that while these childish games were going on, one of the technicians was engaging in very adult games of his own. Each of the girls thought they were the only ones to have him inspect them a little too closely. So he got away with it for a long time. Then one of them finally rounded up some courage and asked another one. Then they asked others. Together, a large group of them approached the staff. There was an investigation and they showed him the door. But the damage had already been done.

* * *

It was common practice when one was upset with a policy to stage a barricade. Many of these had been done before, and the person/people who did them always eventually wound up in solitary.

One day eight of the patients decided to barricade themselves in the one room in the unit that you could not get to by opening a window from the outside. There were four boys and four girls. Rumors are they were taking turns in the bed.

Extra staff from the other units were called in. Talking got them nowhere. Eventually they called in the chief executive of the hospital to talk to them. Still nothing. Negotiations went on well into the morning. Those of us who were not involved were commanded to stay in our rooms with the doors closed.

My roommate (at this time, my roommate was different than the one mentioned above) decided that while the staff was dealing with the barricade problem, it might be a good idea for him to explore homosexuality. He asked me to engage in various sexual activities with him. I respectfully declined his offer.

He eventually gave up and decided if I would not please him, he would please himself. Which he did. Meanwhile, the barricade issue was close to resolved around 3:00 a.m. or so. The staff brought in a chain saw and literally

18

sawed the door down. The eight people inside were taken to the state mental institute in a paddy wagon. I never saw any of them again.

* * *

One standard form of punishment was called an "EBT." This stood for "Early Bed Time." This was used when you did something the staff did not like. Bedtime started at 10:00 p.m. Every EBT was 1/2 hour. And you could, over the course of a day, collect several EBT's on top of each other, thus decreasing your bedtime even more. (I always called these "Extra Bossy Treatment," which was, in my opinion, much more appropriate.)

One fine rebellious day, I was assigned to go to bed at 4:00 p.m. I went into my room and enjoyed the solitude. Hours went by and human nature eventually demanded that I leave my room momentarily. However, the staff completely refused to let me out, as policy clearly stated that once you went into your room for the night, you were, under *no* conditions or circumstances, allowed out until after midnight. And they felt adamant in enforcing that policy this particular evening.

More time went by, and I begged and pleaded to no avail. Eventually I opened the window a crack, resigning myself to the fact that this was the only option I had available to me. (Others who had been in a similar situation had passed this idea on to me long ago, in the event of just such an emergency.)

Being new to this form of dancing, I made the classic neophyte mistake of leaving the bedroom light on. So just as I was using my "unique urinal," one of the male staff happened to be walking by outside. He later came into my room and told me that I may as well have had the spotlight on me in the circus, because that is what it looked like to him.

Staff punished me, and in fact for the rest of my stay there, they never allowed me to fully get back the privileges they took from me.

* * *

For a while during the time I was in the day care program, I was close to a British girl, Mandy. While Mandy and I got along wonderfully, there was also Ellen on the side. Ellen liked me. There were not too many people who were all that nice to Ellen, I was one of the few. Perhaps this was one reason for her infatuation. Be that as it may, I had no romantic interest in Ellen.

19

Mandy and I continued to "date" (to the extent that we could in that situation). It was easy to see that Ellen's jealousy grew ever so slightly every day that Mandy and I were together. Yet Mandy and I still continued to see each other.

One day, after months of flirting and getting nowhere, Ellen just lost her bearings. She was eventually admitted into the inpatient facilities. When I asked why she had been taken there, the response I received was, "Because she became Mandy."

* * *

Just as things hit rock bottom, another patient was assigned to the unit. That would be Lisa. To this day, I feel I owe her a lot. Lisa was a rare find. She was cute, she was compassionate, she was understanding. These are just about the only three qualities I look for in a member of the female persuasion. And if the last two are there, the first one is not important. Inner beauty is far more important to me. Lisa was one year younger than I.

Lisa liked me for some reason. That is okay, because I liked her, too. We spent a lot of time together on the unit. Usually just talking. We both had a need to talk, but neither one of us trusted the staff all that much at this point.

Lisa and I got to know each other very well. And in the process, we kind of helped each other out of our respective shells. Or at least we made it possible to stick our heads out and take a small peep at the world.

Lisa left before I did. I left soon after, to be put into the day care center for a year. Then when I left for good, it was against the better judgment of the staff. They told me I "was not ready" yet. I left anyway. I decided that three years was enough. I had seen enough depression and suicide and all those other things that no one should be forced to witness. There was nothing more for me. Final cost was around $150,000.00. That was many years ago. God only knows what it would be now.

CHAPTER THREE

I Re-Enter the World

Lisa and I stayed in touch with each other, even after I moved to Illinois. I was invited by my aunt and uncle to live with them for a while so I could study computer science at one of the few colleges in the nation that does not require a high school diploma. (I have yet to spend one day, even one hour or minute in high school.) I was working as a veterinary assistant, getting paid only a tiny $3.35 an hour, so I took them up on the offer and moved to Illinois shortly after totaling my father's beloved 1967 Ford Mustang. There are not many things from my past that I still feel guilty about, but this is one of them. Replacing it will be almost impossible. But I hope I get the chance someday.

It should be noted here that while I was in the day care, the world's ugliest stray terrier literally followed me home one day. We decided to keep her. My mother, being big on our roots in Ireland, suggested that I name her "Clancy." Being naturally rebellious, I named her "Mozambique" because that was as far away from anything Irish as I could think of.

Moze was one incredible dog. She always knew what I was thinking or feeling, and she acted accordingly. She was the ultimate perfect personality in a dog for a child with autism. She had other unique qualities. For instance, if I took her for a walk in the park, she would actually climb up the ladder of the biggest slide, and then slide down. She would do this over and over. And the kids in the park really loved it. One fellow even went home to get his video camera to show his wife!

To give this some time reference, We are talking about the fall of 1983. I was 18 years old. Mozambique and I moved to Illinois to try some college classes. I flunked out because I did not understand why the teacher wanted us to do things in his own bizarre fashion. We would have to write code for a program, and he would put an example on the board. I would walk up, erase it, and say to him, "Look, if we did it this way instead, we could save four or five lines of code," and I proceeded to rewrite his code. He said that was true, and it would work, but that he still wanted us to do it his way, and that if I did it my way, I would fail. If I was looking for a job as a programmer, I would not have been hired if I used the code he insisted on. I got frustrated from my confusion, failed the course.

But two very important things happened in my life while I was there that kept it from being a total loss. First, I got my G.E.D., which I hear has gotten significantly more difficult since I took it. I am glad I took the test when I did. And seeing as how I passed it the first time I took it without any studying, it is obvious that I am either very intelligent or I had some divine intervention. Still not sure which it was. The second thing that happened was I made a new friend.

Princess Gwendolyn; she is just what her name implies. She is just about everything you immediately think of when you hear the word "Princess." Her voice is melodic. Her touch is magic. Her looks are incredible. To this day, she remains one of my best friends.

Her compassion is like a flower. Her heartbeat is all of nature. Even when she cannot possibly understand, she somehow understands anyway. I have called her and/or seen her and/or held her when I was scared, crying, depressed, lost, unable to talk, unable to breathe, or just plain wanting to die. She has always been there for me. And she still is. I very strongly believe that without her presence in my life, I would have been dead long ago. And she knows this. I thank God routinely for Gwendolyn. And I care for her even more than she thinks I do.

After the academic failure, I moved back in with my parents in Columbus. I was unable to find suitable employment.

June 15th, 1984. One of the saddest days of my life. I was out cutting the grass in my backyard when my mother came out to tell me I had a phone call. Not knowing what it was, I was grateful for an excuse to stop mowing the lawn for a while. I walked in the house and picked up the phone.

Lisa was dead.

Lisa is gone forever. And I still miss her. I think that the bottom line is that it was obvious to me, even though I was pretty "out of it" at the time, that Lisa was going through a pain very similar to what I was. I think she was just ... sad. Profoundly sad. Sad enough to want to hide from the world, which she did. Sad enough to want to kill herself, which she almost did. Sad enough to ask the questions no one can ever possibly answer. Sad enough to look for reasons, even in the wrong places. Lisa was hurting when I met her, hurting as I was. It was a very similar pain between us. And I think that subconsciously, we both knew that. And that in itself served to make an inseparable bond between us. Only death could do us part. And that is exactly what happened.

22

But before that happened, Lisa was able to lose her pain. She died a happy person. I can take some comfort in that. Maybe it just helps to know that there is at least one other person who suffers as you suffer. No one has a monopoly on pain. We all need to be reminded of this from time to time.

Her death was, to say the least, very hard to handle. My mother, who already knew what the call was, made sure to observe the conversation. Were you to ask, she would tell you that I did not handle it well. But looking back, I do not feel I handled it wrongly. I do not see that it is possible to gracefully handle the news that the person you love more than anyone else in the world is suddenly gone forever. Lisa was 18.

She died in a car accident. She lived in Toledo, and rumors were that she had just gotten a new car and was on her way onto the freeway from the entrance ramp. She never made it. I had talked to her just eight days before. When I hung up the phone, I realized that I forgot to tell her I love her. I put my hand on the phone, then I took it off, thinking I would just be sure to tell her next time. Only there was no next time. Want to know what the biggest mistake I ever made in my life was? Taking my hand back off the phone.

Since there was no employment in sight, I elected to change my major and go back to school. I signed up for the Mental Health Technology program at Columbus State Community College, then called Columbus Technical Institute. Again, I somehow was unable to achieve those high grades.

During this time, Mozambique also died. She was hit by a car. Don't get me wrong, Mozie was a good dog. She knew not to go into the street. But what dog can resist the sight of a possum on the other side of the street? This occurred just as a neighbor down the street was speeding up the street at 40 plus miles an hour, because she was late for her PTA meeting.

This was October 24th, 1984. Just five months after Lisa died. I was devastated. I had just lost the two best friends in my life. But all hope was not lost. God saw fit to compensate me.

That same day Mozambique died (earlier that same day), I had received a postcard in the mail. It was from Gwendolyn, who was at that time just a girl I knew in Illinois. She wondered why I had not written to her. I found that card again as I was deep in depression later that night. I decided I needed someone to talk to, so I called her. The beginning of the conversation (which took place at 3:00 a.m.) went something like this:

RING/RING/RING/RING/RING/RING...

Hello?

Hi, Gwen, this is Tom. Did I wake you up?

Yawn No, you didn't *Yawn* wake me up. What's up? Nice to hear from you!

We talked for a while. And like she has ever since, Gwen listened. I hung up the phone feeling a lot better and I went to sleep. The next day, the phone rang, and I picked it up:

RING/RING...

Hello?

Hello, Tom? This is Gwen. I am calling you because my roommate said you called last night...

It was not her roommate that I talked to the night before, it was Gwen. And whether or not she was telling me the truth that night about being awake, it was that day that Princess Gwendolyn was born.

On May 25th, 1985, Gwendolyn married her sweetheart, Michael. At first, I was a bit angry (or perhaps jealous) about this. But I soon began to see that these two definitely belong together. And Gwen has since made it clear that she will not allow herself to forget about me.

Time went by and my life was basically going nowhere. My father, discouraged that I was not doing anything constructive, got me a job at Medicare. This was in 1986.

On January 13th, I began the job. Now it turns out that I had the world's greatest boss. I have told many people that I have never come across a more compassionate man than Brigadier Weidner. (Although Gwen's husband Michael comes in at a close second.) Compassion is a gift. It is a very beautiful quality to have. But it can also be a hazard in the workplace. The Brigadier was ultimately given another (lower grade) job, and he was replaced. Things went downhill rapidly. This job that I once enjoyed (and thus was somehow able to hang onto), I now hated and despised with a passion. They eventually told me to shape up or ship out. I shipped out. My last day was March 10th, 1989.

But other things happened while I was working there. For instance, my Grandmother turned eighty in 1988, and my mother (her daughter) decided it was time to have a "Let's show Grandma how much we love her party." Her birthday happened to fall on Mother's Day that year, and so Mother arranged to use the Church as a meeting place to throw this wonderful party.

This was a source of stress for me. Having built this up as a major event, I had no idea what to get her as a present. I agonized over this for many days. Then, just two days prior to the party, I finally decided that nothing was worth giving to her if it did not come from my own heart. So I decided I would give her a song for her birthday. But it had to be more than just a song. It had to be something memorable. Special. And I did not know if I could do it. But I had to at least try. So I sat down to write the song, fully aware of the pending party, and of how much I missed my Grandfather at the time. These are the lyrics I came up with:

> *There's a tapestry of time around you now.*
> *You've made a legacy.*
> *People you love surround you now,*
> *love you in harmony.*
> *You've watched your children grow.*
> *Now they have children of their own.*
> *They're all here to see*
> *you turn eighty.*
>
> *You've seen the wars, they've come and gone.*
> *The nation is fairly calm.*
> *No more World War One or Two,*
> *or Korea, or Vietnam.*
> *You watched the death count rise,*
> *it seemed to touch the skies.*
> *Thank God it's history*
> *as you turn eighty.*
>
> *He was a special kind of man.*
> *The kind you don't just come by.*
> *You remember that day he took your hand*
> *and the look he had in his eye.*
> *You want him to be near,*
> *but he just can't be here.*
> *And we all miss his ministry*
> *as you turn eighty.*

25

The future seems like it's here today
and the past feels so very far away,
but that's the mystery
of turning eighty.

You now reflect on the days gone by.
You contemplate the days ahead.
Somehow, it all seems to make you smile
when you remember
what was done, what was said.
You've watched your grandchildren grow,
now they have children of their own.
And they hold you tenderly
as you turn eighty.

The following day, one day before the party, I reported to the recording studio with trusty guitar and Medicare wages in hand. Several hours and $67.73 later, I had my gift.

She loved it. To me, it was just a silly little song that I had written for her, and even today I think I could have done a better job if I had more time to polish it. But that did not seem to matter to her.

Not long after that, she had a stroke. I was not worried, though. She was one feisty woman! And she would get over it. Indeed, as I began to see improvement in my visits to her, yet another stroke hit. Alas, that spelled doom for this woman. For while she did live for a significant period of time after that, it could by no stretch of the imagination be called a "life."

Up to that point, I had never really cared for that song. Yet looking back, I can say that I am glad I recorded it. I feel as though it gave me an opportunity to say "Good-bye." And the scariest thing about all of this that as I watch my mother age, I see more and more of her own mother in her everyday. She claims she does not particularly like this part of herself, but I believe the truth is that she delights in it.

My tour of duty at Medicare over, I went back to school, taking the mental health classes over again. I got A's! But they called me into the office, and again I was kicked out of the technology. They said I was doing fine, academically, but that I was "too young and free-spirited for the helping profession." This can be interpreted an infinite number of ways, and none of them are flattering.

I decided since I was doing okay, I would stay in school anyway. One way to keep my GPA up was to take writing classes. (This was because I have gotten an A on every single essay I have written since going back to school.) I made a switch to journalism, and that is where I am now.

Meanwhile, my younger sister was living in a dormitory while she going to school, and I was still at home. One day I realized my father was financing this. So, mainly as a joke, I said, "Why does Mary get to have a dorm and I have to stay here?" Not expecting a reply, I got one anyway. "You find an apartment, and I will pay for it." I found an apartment. I have been living alone ever since, and loving it! A solitary life is an autistic's dream come true! I wouldn't have it any other way. My thanks to my parents for allowing this.

The first place I lived was in kind of a ratty neighborhood, just a few miles north of downtown Columbus. There were two rooms, a kitchen and bedroom. The bathroom was in the basement.

The rent was a very reasonable $180.00 a month. It had carpeting and it was furnished. I was not really all that happy there, nor did I feel very safe in that neighborhood. But it could have been much worse, and it was a lot quieter than I thought it would be.

Eventually, though, I got into a fight with the landlady. She claimed the cat had given the entire complex fleas. The truth of it was that the stray cat outside was befriended by the girl living upstairs. This cat gave my cat fleas and the fleas spread from there. To me, this indicated it was time to move on.

Searching furiously for alternative low cost housing, I found a place on the campus of the Ohio State University. This was $220.00 a month. My mistake was in picking a place that was right around the campus bars. The other place had been paradise compared to this.

Sirens woke me up every night. Car alarms woke me up every night. Drunk college students fighting over girls in tight jeans woke me up every night. And the worst part of living here was that these same students would take the liberty of urinating on my porch during the late night, bar hopping weekends. There was absolutely no security here. And I felt as though a stray bullet would crash through my window and find me at any moment. I made a note to myself to get out of there at my earliest convenience.

It wasn't until much later that Social Security Eligibility came along and I was able to leave that rat race behind. I am now living in a condominium with emphasis on quiet and security. The two things I had craved for years, I now have in abundance. And I am very happy living here.

But I am getting ahead of myself. After four or five quarters into college, my grades dropped. I guess I was burned out. I quit school. I met a girl, Melanie. I spent many, many days with her, getting to know her better. I spent many, many nights with her, snuggling her close and holding her tight. And so on July 4th, 1990, at 12:20 a.m. I asked her to marry me while we sat naked together in my father's outdoor jacuzzi on a clear night with the stars and full moon smiling down on us. She accepted, and I slid the ring on her finger. It was very romantic, but did not include normal sexual relations.

Five months later, she was raped. Never have I felt such anger. Even Lisa's death did not affect me this way. It would be another four or five nights before I got any sleep. It would be longer before Melanie allowed me (or anyone) to touch her again. We know who did it, but because Melanie panicked, we had no proof. That, combined with the fact that she desperately wanted more from me than I could give her (and perhaps the fact that I am autistic) led to the demise of what seemed the perfect relationship. This was in December, 1990.

CHAPTER FOUR

"Discovering" Autism

Having gone through what I consider the ultimate failure in my life, I decided that there was still something wrong with me and I was determined to figure out what it was. I decided a very close examination of my past was in order. I sat down to write a biography to give some order to this research. I requested my medical records from the hospital. I thought I was ready to read what was on them, but I was in no way prepared to realize that I was autistic. I had studied this ponderous and enigmatic disorder in college. Besides, it doesn't happen to you, only to other people, right? This was in March, 1991.

Actually, the consistent diagnosis was Pervasive Developmental Disability. This ascertainment led me to the medical journals that equated P.D.D. with autism. The probability of autism led me to the Nisonger Center at the Ohio State University where the psychologist confirmed the diagnosis as autism.

But what could have been something tragic turned out to be something beautiful. For once there was a name attached to this problem, I knew there had to be a weapon to fight it. And that weapon, I realized, was knowledge.

Leaving the pain of Melanie behind, at least to the extent that I could, I began to focus all my energies (and waking hours) on acquiring as much knowledge as I could. I consulted as many professionals as I could find, asking them what autism was. I got as many books out of the library as I could and I read them all. I was desperate. I needed to know everything I possibly could about it. Otherwise there was no way that I was ever going to be able to make anything worthwhile come from my life.

One of those books was called "Children With Emerald Eyes." It was written by Mira Rothenberg, and I thought the book was fantastic. Not so much because of the content, though certainly that too, but more because I felt that this woman was a brilliant and gifted writer. I had to find her. I had to talk to her.

My first stop was the publisher. As could be expected, they were no help at all. I tried information, her number was unlisted. I didn't want to write to her, I wanted to *talk* to her.

29

I went back over her book again, looking for any clues I could find about how I could find her. I found a reference to the "Blueberry Treatment Center." I called there and they gave me her number. I called Mira and she was, as usual, very busy. But we talked for a while, after which she told me to go ahead and write to her. So content in having talked to her, and feeling like she *wanted* me to write to her, I politely hung up the phone and settled in to my computer, which back then was an old (but reliable!) CP/M Kaypro 4/84 portable.

Meanwhile I had also been reading *"Autism: A Parents Guide,"* edited by Michael Powers. The back had a listing of references and support groups. One was the *Autism Society of America.* I called all over the States looking for information. Unfortunately, the information he had on it was outdated by the time I had gotten the book.

My search, ironically, eventually led me back to my own hometown of Columbus. I was more than a bit angry with myself for running up the phone bill (more than usual, anyway) for what I could have gotten here locally.

I talked to a fellow who was pretty much just down the street from me. He invited me to attend something called a "local chapter meeting." I had no idea what that was, I had no idea what the ASA was at the time, nor did I ever in my wildest dreams or imagination know of the degree of involvement I would later have with this fine organization. My life was slowly beginning to turn around, starting with the medical records and those two books. But I was completely blind and oblivious to it. I was being bathed by the light, yet I was still walking in darkness.

Then while I was in the middle of writing to Mira, I noticed by the clock on the wall that it was time to go to the local chapter meeting. And so I got in my car and headed for the Childhood League Center, here in Columbus. I was very nervous! Mainly because I was not sure what to say. I knew that I was coming to this meeting only for more information about who ... and what ... I was. And I knew that most of the people there would be coming looking for information about their children. So what do I do? Do I pretend to be a father with an autistic child, or do I admit the truth?

Pretending presented problems because the person who invited me already knew the truth and would hear me flat out lie. The truth was also a problem because I was not sure I wanted the world to know of my diagnosis. With the exception of Gwen, I was always a very private person. I decided I didn't want to make a decision, and I was not going to unless it was forced ᴛ me, at which point I would then decide.

"We have a lot of new faces in the room today. Why don't we start by all of us introducing ourselves?" Great, I thought, they were gonna make me do this. One by one the people made introductions. "Hello, my name is _____ and I have a __ year old child with autism."

The time for my decision had come. I perspired from nervousness. "Hello. My name is Thomas and I ... <insert slight pause for impromptu decision here> ... *am* a child with autism." The room grew silent. I could literally see the jaws drop. There were whispers in the background. "Wow! This is great!" Part of me found this very amusing, yet the rest of me was confused (and somewhat frightened) about what the big deal was.

Question followed question. Most of them I was able to answer. I dominated that meeting. It was certainly not my intention to do so. Indeed, I would have been happy to say nothing at all the whole time. At the end of the meeting everyone wanted to shake my hand and say how happy they were to meet me and that they hoped I would come back the following month. "We need you here," they would say.

Huh? What? Me? *Needed?* Since when? Most people can't wait to get rid of me and now you actually *want me to come back*? What I had been hated and punished for all my life, it was the same thing I was now being *praised* for? It was very confusing! Who were these people who were silly enough to want me to see them again? And the biggest question of all; did I really want to see *them* again? Just how involved did I want to get with this group? What were their beliefs? Where did they stand on the many controversial autism issues I had read about in all those library books? And why did they hold those particular beliefs? I drove home with these questions pervading my mind.

The screen saver was exploding fireworks on my computer when I walked in. I sat down at the terminal and continued writing to Mira, informing her of what had just happened at the meeting. I covered the questions they asked as well as my answers to those questions. And as I was writing, it dawned on me just how much I had learned about autism just in those two short hours I had been away. I realized that I had learned more from those parents than I had during all those hours of reading all those books. And I came to the conclusion that maybe sometimes you can actually learn more by *answering* questions than you can by *asking* them. I puzzled over this for a long time. How can you learn more by answering questions that you already knew the answers to then you can by asking questions you did *not* know the answers to? It didn't make sense! And yet ... that is the way it was.

Due to this discovery, the letter to Mira grew way past what it was originally intended to be. My first goal was to respond to her book. But now my new goal was to try to describe autism as it looked through my eyes. By the time I had finished it, it was 58 pages long. I sent her a copy and I gave a copy to the person who invited me to the meeting. I thought my part in the autism play was over. I thought it was a bit part with no real influence. No one had ever cared what I had to say before. Therefore it was logical to assume that no one cared now. This was August, 1991.

The letter got rave reviews (which I did not know at the time that anyone ever "reviewed" personal mail). Thus it began to pass hands. I was oblivious to this. I mean, I knew it was happening, because there were a few people who called me or wrote to me to ask permission (which I always gave, not because I was thrilled about strangers reading about my life, but because I was so flattered that someone thought I actually had done something of *value*), but most people just read it and gave it to someone else to read. I did not know the extent to which it was happening.

It was not long before mail started coming into my campus apartment and into my parents home. A lot of it, from all over the country (and on occasion, other parts of the world). All of them thanking me for the "manuscript." I did not know that at the time all they had was Temple's book and a few *Advocate* articles. I did not know how in demand this kind of insight and information was. And no one was more surprised than I was.

How could it be that something that made me such a bad person was now making me a *good* person? I really struggled with this, even as more mail (and phone calls) came in.

After much pondering, I realized it was unlikely that I was ever going to understand what was really happening, and that the easiest way to handle it would be to simply enjoy it. I went back to the mail and answered it as best I could. I also wrote two more letters to Mira and packaged them together as the Mira Trilogy. There are copies all over the world, and those letters are the basis of this book.

I had seen in the past that sometimes this kind of thing can "go to a person's head." And I did not want that to happen to me. One thing I decided to do to avoid it was occasionally do some kind of "servant labor" to keep my head grounded in reality. I would volunteer at a counseling center or maybe spend the night with the homeless. I still do this, though not as much as I used to. Nevertheless, two people whom I had considered friends for a very long time began to see what was happening. I was under the impression that this was the kind of thing that you share with your friends. If you don't, then what is the purpose of friendship? I told them everything that had happened, and how it surprised me and how confused I was by it. "Wow," they'd say, "you are getting famous!" Yet instead of being proud of me like friends should, and supporting me like friends should, they decided for some reason that they did not want to be my friends anymore. That is the impression that I have anyway, as they have not called me or visited me in several months. I miss them both. But while I was losing old friends, I was gaining new friends. And these new friends, unlike the old friends, had an idea what autism was, and so they understood Thomas much better than the old friends. Maybe it was not so bad after all.

After a few meetings of the local chapter of ASA, it was suggested to me that I may want to run for the national board of directors. My response was to laugh. "Shyeah, right. As if!" Okay, so I wrote something about autism and I answered a few simple questions. Big deal. Anyone can do that. I am not special. Nor am I national board material. I wouldn't last a minute on the board. I would be thrown off in disgrace. And I had certainly already had enough embarrassment and pain in my life. I didn't need anymore.

But then this person (and others joined him) began telling me otherwise. "*Not* everyone could do it. You *are* special. You have come out of your autism and that is just not done. What I would not give for my child to be like you! You are a miracle. And I am pleased, and proud, very proud, to know you. And to be able to call you my friend."

What? I came out of it? I am a miracle? This was a lie! If this was true then my parents would not have punished me all those times they did. If this was true then they would be *proud* of me!

I needed to investigate this to see if there was any truth to it at all. I called Mira, who basically told it was all true, every word. And I called Gwen. Though she had no idea what autism was, she also seemed to agree. (Which made me ask myself exactly what kind of evolution she had seen in me since I had first met her.) I read more books, I read more articles, I talked to more professionals. There seemed to be a ring of truth to what they said. Maybe I was quite a bit better off than I believed.

Still, I wanted no part of the national board. It was not for me. Fly around the country? Sit in a room full of strangers all day? Voting on complex issues? No no no! What if I ... um ... made a mistake? What then? Was not worth the risk. I respectfully declined. I couldn't do it. I was just too scared. And I was not worthy of being on a national board. That was for *really* special and important people, not me.

Meanwhile, I continued reading everything I could on autism. But it was not enough. Books were books, and books had knowledge. But I had discovered at that first local chapter meeting that I learn better by talking to people than I do by reading a book. Then it dawned on me that perhaps one solution would be to join the national board. Who else would know more about what autism was or what was going on in the field or the various therapies used to treat it than the board members? This was knowledge I craved! I decided that the least I could do was explore the possibility. After all, I was under no obligation, right?

I got a call from Youngstown, Ohio. They were inviting me to the local chapter meeting. I took the offer because I wanted to meet more people who knew about autism. They told me there was going to be a guest speaker who had autism and had just written a book. I was quite jealous. I personally thought I was a damn good writer. Why was I not asked to write a book? Still, it would be a thrill to actually meet someone else like myself. I had never done that before. My car broke down *just* as I pulled into the center where the meeting was. I walked in and sat down next to the guest of honor. His name (very much unknown at the time) was Sean Barron. Later, the book written by Sean and his mother--*"There's A Boy In Here"* would be a best seller.

I liked this guy immediately. There was something really special about him. Perhaps it was the fact that I saw more of myself in him than in anyone else I had ever met. Both of us spoke to the group. Something neither of us had ever done before. (And here, I would like to pause to say that as we have both gone on to be successful speakers, I am very proud to have shared that first talk for both of us with him. Though I do not see him or talk to him as much as I would like to, I do consider Sean to be a friend.)

After a nightmare getting my car repaired, I came back to Columbus to find a check for $100.00 in the mail. The check stub said "Speaker's Fee" on it. Now they were *paying* me just to *talk* to them? Something that I felt I needed to do anyway? I wondered if maybe I might be onto something here. And that check made the decision about the board of directors an easy one. I called several people and I asked them to nominate me for the board of directors. I needed three nominations. I made sure the board got six.

I filled out the form and I sent it in. Up until three days before the votes were tallied, I believed I would be elected. Then I began to get nervous.

And I could not decide which would be worse. To be elected or to *not* be elected. That was the question. Then the ASA president at the time called me one night around 11:30 p.m. and left a message on my answering machine telling me that I had indeed been elected. He invited me to attend the national conference in Albuquerque. Not long after, Julie Donnelly, who had read the letter(s) to Mira, invited me to speak on the panel of adults with autism at the conference.

Speaking at a local chapter meeting was one thing. Speaking at a national conference was something else entirely. What had happened to me? Why was all this happening? And if I had married Melanie, would any of it have happened then? I began to realize (for the first time) that maybe it was *okay* that Melanie and I had split up. It was beginning to appear as though it may not be the end of the world after all.

Albuquerque was wonderful. The weather was perfect. The mountains were perfect. The conference was perfect. They could not have picked a better place if they had tried. The day before the conference, I walked from my hotel to the convention center to look it over. I figured I could easily get away with this. I was a national board member now. Who was going to stop me?

There was another conference going on, the "International Association of Gay Square Dancers." This took me by surprise. Though after I spent a few more days in Albuquerque, I saw that it really should not have. (One thing that makes Albuquerque so wonderful is the cultural diversity.) I walked around the conference for a while, a couple guys came on to me, I saw some good square dancing, and my favorite part of the whole thing was buttons they were selling that said, "Dip me in chocolate and throw me to the lesbians!" I was sorely tempted to buy one for a gay friend of mine.

I spent most of the conference looking for William Christopher. I had heard he was going to be there and I wanted to meet him. I had long admired M*A*S*H, and Father Mulcahy was pretty much the reason. I saw Mulcahy as the man who quietly and in the background (almost unnoticed) was in reality the glue that held the 4077th together. I admired this about him. He gave so much of himself to the 4077th, yet he asked very little in return. He seemed to be content just doing God's work. That is all that mattered to him. You have admire a faith like that. I had often wondered who the man was behind the character.

I finally found him out in the hall one evening on his way to a get together hosted by the Devereux Foundation. This was invite only and I did not have an invitation. Gary Mesibov, the executive director of the well-respected T.E.A.C.C.H. program of North Carolina, bless his little Gary heart, arranged for me to crash the party. But I soon felt woefully out of place. All the big names in autism were in this room. What in the world was *I* doing here? They were all wearing suits and ties and here I was wearing jeans. I felt very much overwhelmed. Here in this room, legends gathered. I felt as though I was surrounded by greatness. Authors, professionals, advocates (sometimes one person was all three), people who would forever be known for the incredible work they did to advance the cause of autism and to improve the lives of countless children. It was then that the implications and responsibility of being a board member hit me. And it was then that I wanted to go home.

I didn't think I could ever possibly adjust. I thought the pressure and responsibility would be too great. I stood in awe of Temple Grandin and all that she had done. How could I ever match up to this woman? How could I ever stand in her shoes? How could I ever do what she did? How could I ever be the advocate that she was? I was very fortunate to find the answer, though it did take some searching. And even so, I sometimes still wonder if I will ever be the advocate that she is. She is truly a remarkable woman.

Skip ahead one year to the 1993 International Conference in Toronto. The previous year I had been traveling extensively, attending board meetings and speaking at conferences.

Then one day I opened my closet and found the old guitar gathering dust as it had been doing for so long. I picked it up and played some of the songs I wrote. I sighed to myself as I realized those songs had all been written a lifetime ago. I was someone else now. Not the person who wrote this music.

I sat down to write a song about autism, thinking it may be interesting to see if a way could be found to successfully blend music and advocacy. And what I discovered, much to my horror, was that whatever that ability was to write songs years ago, it was gone now. I had to actually *struggle* to write the song. Something I had never had to do before. And even then, it wasn't all that great:

Build Me A Bridge

I have known that you and I
have never been quite the same.
And I used to look up at the stars at night
and wonder which one was from where I came.
Because you seem to be part of another world
and I will never know what it's made of.
Unless you build me a bridge, build me a bridge,

build me a bridge out of love.

I long for the day that you smile at me
just because you realize
that there's a decent and intelligent person
buried deep in my kaleidoscope eyes.
For I have seen the way that people look at me
though I have done nothing wrong.
Build me a bridge, build me a bridge,
and please don't take too long.

Living on the edge of fear.
Voices echo like thunder in my ear.
See me hiding every day.
I'm just waiting for the fear to lift away.

I want so much to be a part of your world.
I want so much to break through.
And all I need is to have a bridge,
a bridge built from me to you.
And I will be together with you forever,
and nothing can keep us apart.
If you build me a bridge, a tiny, little bridge
from my soul, down deep into your heart.

The song lacked the "magic" of the other songs I had written. I went back to those songs and tried to identify that magic and I failed. The only thing that made those songs good was that the person who wrote them had a talent, an ability to write good music. That person is gone now. And I have taken his place. However, as a tribute to him, whoever and wherever he is, I have included some of his best work in the back of this book.

I was not really happy with my scheduled time to speak at the Toronto conference. I was to be the last speaker of the conference. I felt bad because I knew that by the time people got to me, they would be burned out from days of conferencing. I wanted to ease that fatigue. I wanted to do something that would be memorable and easy. Something to take their mind off of the past few days. And I wanted it to be casual so they didn't have to take notes like they had been doing all week.

So I played the song. (What most people don't know is that I actually wrote that last verse in the hotel room a few hours before my presentation.) When my talk was over, everyone went immediately to the tape counter because they wanted a copy of my song. A song that I thought (and still think) was rather insignificant. The purpose in playing it was just to give a breather to burned out conference goers. Now Toni Flowers is using it as background music for a slide show presentation she does and Diane Twachtman is using it in therapy with her clients with Aspergers. I have also heard that no tape sold more copies the entire conference than that one did. I consider this to be an achievement. Not bad for the last speaker at an international conference.

CHAPTER FIVE

What Autism is to Me

Here are some views about autism from my perspective inside the maze. I'd like to elaborate on just a few things.

Speech. Speech is hard for me. I can make people think I am "normal," but it takes much effort and energy. Some times more than others. These times seem to fluctuate at random unless stress is involved. There are, on occasion, still times when I want to talk, but I can't. I can try and try and try, but I can't talk. There is a fear holding me back. I do not know what it is I am afraid of, I only know that it is a feeling of fear unlike any other feeling of fear I have ever known. It is not that I do not want to talk, it is that I am *unable* to at that moment. I was asked by a parent once why it seems her child can talk fine at some times and why he cannot talk at all during other times. Many people have scratched their heads trying to figure this out. I'd like to offer this theory, based on personal experience.

I believe that fear is the dominant emotion in autism. People with autism do not usually *know* what it is that they are afraid of and I think this is the result of sensory overload. They can trust no one. But... there are times when things are so quiet and so placid, times when there is next to zero sensory stimuli, or times when they are so wrapped up in whatever activity they may be doing at the moment, that the fear fades. Just for a little bit. I believe this is when they decide to talk. Either that, or they are, at the moment, fighting one incredible war with the demons whirling within them. And even if they just say one little thing, it is a victory of sorts and they are in a sense winning the battle. And we should all be very, very proud of them. Because what they did was not easy. And it takes a very strong person to fight it.

Change. I hate change. I always have, I always will. Change is inevitable. And I realize this. Nothing is going to stay the same forever. But while things are the same, there is a feeling of security. You know where and when and how and sometimes even why everything is. Then when it changes, it forces you to readjust, something I have never found easy to do. And sometimes this fear of change is strong enough that the mind plays some nasty tricks.

For instance, if I am out doing my grocery shopping, the way I usually do it is to first allot myself a set amount of money, then buy groceries up to that amount, tallying the price as I go along. I round up so as to be sure I have

39

enough money, then when I get close to whatever the amount is, I head for the checkout line. This is probably the way most people do it.

The problem comes in the line. As the cashier is punching in the prices and asking me that God awful "Will that be paper or plastic this evening, Sir?" I never know how to answer that question, I am suddenly overcome with this terror that the prices are somehow "different" or "changed" now that I am paying for them, and that I am going to be very *embarrassed* because I will have to choose what not to buy. (Very similar to the way Sean Barron used to open and close the doors over and over to make sure they all went to the same place as the last time he looked.) Now I know this fear is totally irrational. So I try to calm myself by just reminding myself that according to the physical laws of the universe, it is not possible for the prices to change from point A, the shelf, to point B, the register. This rarely works, and I sweat it through. In all those times I have gone grocery shopping, I think I have underestimated only once. But that doesn't seem to help, either.

I have heard this is a common problem. I am not sure how this can be since it would mean that a simple thing like shopping is a terror for everyone.

Sleep. Sleep is difficult. It is hard to go to sleep and then it is hard to stay asleep. But I have found a few things that help.

A friend of mine once came over and decided to stay the night. He borrowed one of the bears off of my bed and told me, *"If you can't sleep with a woman, a bear is the next best thing."* And I couldn't agree more. My bed is full of bears.

Every time I travel, a bear travels with me. During the 1993 International Autism Conference in Toronto, a couple of people decided to sneak into my room to look around. I heard it was because they wanted to know what a higher functioning autistic person's hotel room would look like. (?) The first thing they saw was the bear on the bed. They thought it was ... "appropriate." They didn't touch anything, just looked around and left. I did not hear about it until later, but I found it very amusing that they wanted to peek in.

Heat is very important to me. I can't get to sleep if it is cold. I used to have an electric blanket that I used every night, even in the Summer. When I was young, my parents could not understand why I always had the blanket on. (They were always afraid it would start a fire.) It was not all the way up, level II or III is where I usually had it. I just wanted to be comfortable, and that was one way that I could do it. Now I have a waterbed that was given to me, and I have it set usually between 95 and 100. Sometimes higher.

40

Sometimes no matter what, I still can't sleep. In these cases, I take either Actifed or Benedryl. Or sometimes Nyquil. I have tried various official "sleeping medicines," but none of them work for me. Anti-histamines knock me right out. But it usually has to be a stronger dose than what is recommended. I *only* do this as a last resort. I have also found that in many cases it helps to cry myself to sleep.

Waking up is usually no easier than falling asleep. It is almost like the mind and body are "out of phase" with each other. It takes a few minutes for me to come back into focus. Moving or being active before then is something I find to be very painful.

One thing I have done to make it easier is to get a talking alarm clock. You push the button on top of the clock and a female voice tells you the time. *"It is: nine thirty three, ay emm."* I find it easier to move my finger over to tap the button than I do to try to focus my eyes. I have been called "lazy" for doing this. But that is not the way it is. I do it this way so I do not feel the need to scream.

Libido. I have no libido. None. This often makes it very hard to relate to other guys when they talk about such things (which is frequently, it seems). They are constantly looking at the girls walking down the street with lust in their eyes. I do not understand this. I appreciate beauty as much as the next guy. And if a girl is cute, I will think to myself, "She is cute." But that is all I will think. There is nothing that man, woman, child or beast could do to get me interested. This also proved to be a problem with Melanie. I had no problem with holding her. She wanted more than that. I was simply unable to give it to her. I am not so sure I could've kept my promise to consummate the marriage, either. The drive/desire is just not there.

New Year's Eve, 1991. I go to a party at friend Brandy's house in Reynoldsburg, Ohio. (I won't get into what happened during the party, just try to imagine your standard NYE party and you will probably get the idea.) The crowd began to thin out and Brandy went into the bedroom to lie down. I went into the bedroom to lie down next to Brandy. Brandy's daughter came in to lie down next to me. Time goes by and her daughter eventually falls asleep holding my hand. Brandy puts her head on my shoulder and falls asleep. So here I am, this guy, lying in this bed, with a fairly attractive woman sleeping on each side of me. I lift up my head and take a look at these two sleeping, and I think, "Man, I know some guys who would *kill* to be in this situation!" But I felt nothing like that. It was nice to have these two to snuggle, but that is as far as I wanted to go with both of them. I tried to imagine what it would be like to "want" either (or both) of them, as I suspect most any other guy in that position would, and I found it to be just a wee bit on the repulsive side. Brandy is cute. So is Kristin. But just because they are cute does not mean I am going after them. It just means they are cute.

Appetite. Along with a lack of libido, there is a lack of appetite. What is hunger? I am not sure I know. I rarely, if ever, feel a need to eat anything. And there are very few foods I can eat without getting very sick. This has been a problem for me on more than one occasion. Mainly at social gatherings. The fact that people with autism sometimes have aversions to certain foods is well documented. And I am no exception. So it would be infinitely easier to tell you what I do like than to tell you what I do not like. Pizza tops the list. The pizza must be simple. Preferably cheese, although I can handle pepperoni in social situations when called for. I also like hot dogs and hamburgers. Both must be without the bun, as I find that the bun ruins the taste. Also, if possible, I like a slice or two of cheese on them. Preferably cheese of the Swiss persuasion. I like macaroni and cheese (homemade is better than store bought!) and noodles romanoff and fettucini alfredo. These must also be simple, without tuna or anything mixed in. I like mashed potatoes (real are better than instant) and I like my mother's own brand of deviled eggs and meat loaf. But then, so do a lot of people. I like milk, white, not chocolate, and I like Kool-aid (lemonade, orange, grape, wild cherry, and purplesaurus rex, which I was making before they thought of it) and I like Hawaiian Punch. Ribeye steak is also very yummy, but I never did care much for T-bone. That about covers it. Although I am sure I left a few things out. And there are two foods in particular that I absolutely despise and will never eat again as long as I live. These would be liver and lima beans. (And who can blame me?)

Potty Training. I have heard many parents tell me that their kids with autism seem to have problems being potty trained. I would ask that these parents take into consideration the possibility of a pain factor. I had this problem growing up, and one of the main reasons was because it hurt like hell.

Family. I have told many people, only half in jest, that "I come from a very strange family." My parents are certainly no exception to this.

Mother claims adamantly to have had no medical confirmation of my autism. In fact, she says she did not know it until I told her. (My father says the same thing.) Seems to me that with all those doctors I went to as I was growing up, and the consistent reference to P.D.D., at least one of these "experts" would have put the puzzle together and used the word autism and would have told her *something*, yes?

42

Mother loves sports. I know that I can always find her in her favorite chair in the living room, watching a game on ESPN and knitting a hat or blanket or afghan for a friend or family member. I do not share her affinity for sports. The one small commonality I have is that I am always glad to hear when the Reds win. But now that Pete Rose is gone, even that is not really important to me. (Pete was one of my heroes, until he ...)

Things were very different long ago. Yet time has skewed my memory and I am no longer sure *how* things were different. I only know that since I have returned from the institution, my relationship with her has dramatically changed. I would personally like to see it improve, but as time has gone by, I have resigned myself (as I believe she has) to the fact that it may never happen.

One problem I have with her is that everything was my own fault and I was a bad child. Or at least that is the way she made me feel. Or perhaps that is what she was told by the powers that be. I thought that everyone had these problems that I do, and that I was just for some reason unable to handle them as well as everyone else. Finally finding the diagnosis was a weight off my shoulders.

In her defense (and it would not be fair to publish this book without saying this), it may in some ways be good that she never knew of the correct diagnosis. Because in all that punishment I received growing up, I was forced into learning how to emulate "normal." I was not normal then and I am not normal now. But I think I can fake it when I absolutely need to. And it was because she made me learn how to that I can. I may owe her something for that.

This brings us to my father. Like my mother, he, too, does not seem to have a clear grasp at all of the demons within me. But he tries to be understanding, and he seems to have a strong desire to help me out. Whenever an *Advocate* or some other newsletter comes to the house, he is the first to read it. Sometimes I think there is nothing he will not do for me. And I think that sometimes he does not see that I appreciate this, but really I do. I value this about my father. He not only loves me, but he loves all of his children. And he likes to make sure we know it from time to time.

My father has many uncanny abilities. Among them (and my personal favorite, as it is absolutely incredible to watch) is the fact that this man can look at a car and whatever was wrong with the car will now be right again. It is truly amazing. He doesn't have to do anything to the car. Just look under the hood, and maybe occasionally very lightly jiggle a few wires and then the cars runs again. Unfortunately, it took me a long time to see that he could do this, so I missed out on observing this when I was young.

All of which brings me to my oldest brother, Charlie. I am slowly beginning to have a great amount of respect for this man, my brother. First, he has five kids, now between ages six and eleven. I do not know how he does it! One of them is not his, but he has legal custody at the moment. Justin (who has just turned four) is the son of Ruth's niece. (Ruth is his wife, of course.)

Charlie is developing a strong Christian faith. And through these five kids that I love and adore so very much, I am beginning to develop that type of brotherly relationship that should have been there long ago. Perhaps this is a step toward my father's dream of seeing his family reunited. But if so, it is only one small step of many that must be taken. And I will say also that of every member of my family, Ruth is (and probably will always be) the one that I love and trust the most. She accepts me for who I am. And it is very hard for me to find that elsewhere in the family.

This brings me to James, my other brother. But there is nothing I can say about him. I have not seen him for 13 years. And there is no indication that I am going to be seeing him anytime soon. This is sad. For if my father's dream of a united family is to come true, the first thing that must happen is for the prodigal son to return.

And so we come to Mary. Sweet, cute, intelligent, charming, and perfect Mary. My younger sister. The only one in the family who never caused any real problems. She was always a little angel. She continuously got A's in school. Grade school, high school, college, even. She has a degree in education, and now has a successful career. I wish I could say the same about me!

Other family relations include Bing Crosby on my mother's side and my namesake, Thomas McKean, whose name you will find on the Declaration of Independence, on my father's side.

And that just about covers the family end of things. All the financial support a person with autism could dream of, but a little less emotional support. I have learned long ago to go elsewhere for this. The emotional support is getting better, though, as the family learns more about what autism is. Maybe this book will help.

Society's Reactions. I have always been interested in society's reactions to autism, and to society's reactions to Thomas. Both are fascinating.

44

For example, people used to tease me about having no sex drive. They called me names and did other cruel things. Then AIDS came along and that attitude changed. Now they say they wish they were like me and not a slave to their hormones.

I have had many people ask me how they could "become autistic." It is laughable (almost) that one would go so far as to wish this on one's self. As with all people, there is more to Thomas than what they see on the surface, but it would appear that sometimes people forget to take this into consideration. Yet while I do not particularly desire a cure, I would also like to be a wee bit more "normal" than I am. And I have never denied that one reason I am doing the advocacy is because I'm not qualified to do anything else.

A companion would certainly make life a little easier. And I hear all the time people tell me that "someday" I will find that someone special. Personally, I have given up hope of that happening. And I am not sure that I have time for a relationship just now. I have seen that I certainly have enough of my own problems to deal with, without worrying about anyone else's. Perhaps when those problems are solved, I will start looking. For now, I am putting all my energy into the advocacy, in hopes of correcting my mistakes and becoming a better advocate, and getting more accomplished. My current companion is the letters and calls I get from parents and professionals, and the countless library books I curl up to read. I crave knowledge. But I have learned schools are not all that cooperative. So I try to teach myself as best I can and at my own pace. This seems to be working. My only regret is that by going this route, I will likely not ever get that piece of paper called a "degree" which is so important in our society.

I'd like to think I'd make a good husband for someone. While I was with Melanie, I was completely loyal to her. Unlike her ex-husband, I never had any desire to be with anyone other than her. That is how special she was and that is how much she meant to me. But I have seen that love is not written in the stars for Thomas. Or perhaps it would be better to say that being *in love* is not written... Any relationships I have are fine as long as we remain just friends. And in some cases those friendships grow far stronger than the friendships that most people have. Yet every time some romance has been introduced into the equation, that relationship ultimately fizzles out and dies. So I have learned to work on building strong friendships, and I let it go at that. And if sexual feelings for another person are a prerequisite for being in love, then it may well be that I will never know what this feels like. It may be that to be in love is simply beyond my ability.

45

People often ask me what autism is when I tell them what I am doing for a living. I am amazed at the lack of knowledge on the part of the general population. The best example of this I can give is a jacuzzi party I had for some friends one year while my parents were out of town. It was Halloween and a friend was celebrating a birthday. One bozo decided to pour dish soap into the jacuzzi. All of a sudden I look down and there are all these bubbles. So I walk into the living room where the same guy notices all the bubbles on me. He stared at me, fixated on something. I knew he was looking at something, but I had no idea what it was.

"Flex your muscles," he said. So I did and he was fascinated. It turns out that *he* thought that part of autism was some kind of skin disfigurement and that the bubbles on my arms were actually a part of *me*.

The following story is another illustration of how society misunderstands autism.

"A little traveling music..."

Once, while I was doing some work for Jackie Rockwell, I was required to go to Monroe, Louisiana. On the way back home to Columbus, some odd things began to happen.

I was showed into the aircraft personally by a flight attendant before anyone else was allowed to board. The flight attendants would occasionally come to my row and ask me if I was okay. (They called me by name, too!) This happened two or three times. There was a lady sitting next to me and the last time it happened, she looked at me kind of funny. So I said to her, "Why do you think they are treating me like some kind of ... ?" The last word popped into my head *just* as I got to it: "Rain Man."

And all of a sudden it was very clear to me what was going on. Jackie had informed them at the airport that I was autistic and to watch out for me. And watch out for me is what they did!

The plane made a stop in Florida and I got off to look around the airport. I was walking down the ramp and I was stopped by a flight attendant. "Mr. McKean? Are you aware that this is not Ohio? We are in Florida!" I assured her that I knew and I went on my way. But I did not get completely in the gate until that action was repeated by someone else who pretty much demanded I stay on the aircraft.

I got back on the plane again. They continued to give me the kid glove treatment. The plane had a three-hour layover in the Atlanta, Georgia airport.

When the plane landed, there was an announcement that everyone was to stay in their seats. The reason for this turned out to be so I could be escorted off the plane first. Looking back, I am still not sure how I felt about it. Was I happy that I did not have to wait for everyone to get their belongings from the overhead bin (which may have shifted during take off or landing), or was I angry (not to mention embarrassed) that they were making all this fuss over me?

I tried to tell them I did not need an escort. They smiled and said of course I didn't, and escorted me anyway. When I got to the gate, there was the standard fellow there giving information on connecting flights. We got to the gate and the flight attendant said, "We have an autistic gentleman here. Please take care of him."

The response, "I know, ma'am, I *have* been briefed." He turned to me and said, "Stand behind me, Sir. Please don't move." I stood behind him, not moving, until every last person got off that plane and he gave the connecting information. I began to get irritated at this point. Why was I to get off first if I was to be served last? Didn't make any sense to me.

When everyone had gone on their way, he turned to me as if asking himself what to do with me. Just at that moment, one of the shuttles was going past. This was your typical airport shuttle service requiring a woman with PMS to drive the shuttle. The man explained to her that I was an individual with autism (she already knew), and that I was to go to gate B-11 (which *I* already knew). She took me to gate B-11.

She informed the man at the terminal that I was a person with autism and to look after me. (He also already knew I was coming.) He took my boarding pass, did whatever they do to them, and told me to have a seat. At this point, I started to get a little miffed. I was *not* going to sit in an uncomfortable seat for three hours while there was an entire airport to explore! But what to do about it?

I sat there for a good 10 or 15 minutes trying to plan an escape from what was fast becoming an intolerable situation. Not only did I want to get away from this guy, but the possibility of a game of "cloak and dagger" intrigued me. Of course the first thing that would come to anyone's mind at this point is to make up a story about how you have to go to the bathroom. But when I pondered this, I realized I would most likely be escorted there, too. So that idea was out.

The man turned around the corner of the counter for just a second. It was now or never. I grabbed my carry-on and as quietly and as quickly as I could, I ran around the corner of the hall. How to keep them finding me? Go to another concourse! I ran to the "C concourse" and relaxed. I found a little bar and I sat way in the back and ate a pizza. Then I walked around the stores for a while. The thought occurred to me that it felt very similar to the restrictions placed on me in the institution. It was not a pleasant thought.

But eventually it was time for the plane to take off again for Columbus, and time for me to go back to face the music at B concourse. I wondered, as I was walking back, to what extent they tried to find me. Did the guy just shake his head and get on with his life? Did he call security? Was the entire airport security on alert? No, that was paranoid and grandiose thinking. Or was it?

No sooner did I arrive on B concourse than I was literally surrounded by a large group of security. One of them asked me if I was Thomas McKean and I made the mistake of being honest with him. He grabbed his walkie talkie and said, "This is Charlie Niner. Target has been located. I repeat: target has been located!" The response from the walkie: "Roger, Charlie Niner. Good job! Over and out." Never having been a "target" before, I found the whole experience very interesting.

I was flanked by security as we walked back to B-11. I felt like some kind of rock star or president who had a threat on his life. A flight attendant grabbed me rather tightly by the arm and escorted me onto the plane. This was about ten minutes before anyone else was allowed to board. I figured they just didn't want to lose me again. The guy at the gate gave me one of the nastiest looks I have ever seen as I walked by, as if he were to receive a reprimand for letting me leave his sight. That thought made me smile. Because this whole thing was ridiculous.

The flight attendants spent that ten minutes teasing me about whether I was married or not. (Yeah, like they were really interested or something.) Then, when we got to Columbus, I was once again escorted off the plane and "delivered" to the person waiting for me.

Naturally, the first thing I did when I got home was to call Jackie and relay this whole embarrassing story to her. She told me that the reason she said something to the airport was that the other person with autism who was traveling with us liked to have that extra attention. I told her I would be quite happy without it. The situation has been worked out. I am now once again just another passenger. And that is the way I like it.

Another very quick example of the public's ignorance of autism I can give is a fellow who was talking to me and said, "Huh? Autistic? What is that? Is that like Autistic Fibrosis?"

As hard as it may be to believe, all of these stories are true. And they all point out a desperate need for education.

Computers. These are a god-send to the autistic population. Especially the field of telecommunications. Public message bases and private mail are easier for me to communicate with because I don't have to use all that energy trying to talk in a normal manner. I can just type in silence. This cuts down drastically on sensory overload. On systems with multiple lines, it provides an ideal atmosphere to observe social interaction without leaving the home. I have found that the situation that I am most comfortable in is one where I am with others and alone at the same time. Unfortunately, there are not many ways that it can be done. But this is one of them.

Herein also lies the easiest way to contact the author. Those of you who have a modem may dial 614-338-8400, 614-846-7669 or 614-486-3311 and ask for *Starchild*. (Appropriate name, yes?) You will find me there.

Wandering. It seems as though there are some children with autism who are, as the parent put it, "master escape artists." This is something that they do not understand, but something that I personally understand all too well. This ability to escape should not be looked upon as a bad thing. It seems a lot of parents feel this way about it. They turn around and he is gone. Where did he go? Panic sets in. But this is a skill necessary for survival. It was never anything I *wanted* to do, it was instead something I very much *needed* to do. Bottom line; I had no choice! There is a need; a drive to hide, to retreat, to get away from it all. To find a place quiet and tranquil. I never knew where I was going, but I knew I was there when I arrived. And to be kept by the parent from doing that would be both a horror and a terror that go far beyond the realm of the imagination. If your child needs to get away, support him in doing so. This is not to say that you can't go with him, you can find a quiet place to take a "time out" with him if necessary. And if you find that place and he wants to be alone, let him be alone. Trying to find some way of understanding this would definitely be one of the best things the parents could ever do for the children.

Nerves. My nerves are dead. They have decayed and crumbled inside my body until there is nothing left but the shell of where they used to be. I do not know the meaning of the word "calm." That word is as alien to me as "lust" and "hunger." I go to the beach, and I see these girls in bikinis all decked out on the beach, asleep, getting a nice tan. It amazes me that they can allow themselves the freedom to do that. To maybe be hurt.

I find I am on guard at all times. The only time I am not is when I am with only the closest friends. And even then, the shields never go all the way down. For if they were to go all the way down, I would be forced to retreat against my will into the world I created for myself long ago. A world where everything is okay, and there is no reality. By setting up these defenses, the children are only protecting themselves. And I feel that they have every right to do that.

Withdrawal. I have been trying, as I have been writing this, to come up with a way to describe that curious, withdrawn, "other world." I have been unable to do so. Again, I suspect it is because I have nothing to compare it to. Sight is different, sound is different. I cannot tell you how they are different, because the only sight and sound most have experienced are the sight and sound of the standard variety. Touch is different, too. Just because you are feeling something does not mean it is there. Taste and smell are the same way. If I was to try to come up with a way to describe it, the best I could do would be "*Distorted.*" And while that helps you a little, it really does not help you all that much. I have learned that my five senses are dysfunctional, and they do not always tell me what is going on, and they are not always reliable.

Social Interactions. Humanity is basically nothing but one big enigma to me. What is it that drives people to do what they do? Why does the same not apply to me? What can I do to better fit in with mainstream society? These are questions I am currently (and constantly) asking myself. I have had limited success in answering them. I think I have found a possible solution. I have lately been very careful to observe society and interaction. There are many ways that people communicate and many things that they do while they are together that simply make no sense to me. Sometimes I make a note of these things I see, and then I contact someone who knows me well enough to answer my question about it in a way that I can understand. Unfortunately, there are not many people who fit that description. Perhaps someday I will go on to have more than just limited success in this area. I would like that very much.

Aversives. While I can't sit here and tell you how to raise or treat your kids, I do want to take a moment to say that I am very opposed to the use of punitive measures or aversives. These were occasionally used in the institution and they did the exact opposite of what they were supposed to do. It was not until someone with a little compassion and common sense came along that I began to make progress.

50

I believe that most (if not all) of the behavior seen in autism comes from sensory integration dysfunction. For instance, a person may not want to wear clothes because they find a certain type of material painful. Or they may not want to go to a certain place because the noise echoes in their ears. You, on the other hand, do not realize this because they can't tell you. And they can't tell you because they are either unable to communicate it to you or they do not know that what they are experiencing is abnormal. So it is assumed in many cases to be deviant behavior. And by using aversives to change the behavior, you are only treating the symptoms while the root problems remain.

Therefore I would like to suggest an alternative. If one is considering aversives, one might also consider taking the child to an occupational therapist who is both trained and certified (make sure this person is *certified*) in the use of sensory integration. If possible, or if the child has violent tendencies, find an OTR/L who has had previous experience in dealing with the autistic population. Have the child evaluated and treated.

In this way, one is not only treating the child in a more humane fashion, but also getting to the core of the problem, which will ultimately yield better results.

Self Stimulation. I will be the first to admit that I find spinning objects fascinating. It has a rather pleasing effect on the eyes. I like to occasionally spin a quarter or a penny, play with a top, or watch the wheels spin on a car. My grandfather had two tops that when you spun them, they would flip over and keep spinning. They were given to me when he died, and I still have them. Even all these years later. I also like magnetism and gravity. I find these two things as fascinating as spinning objects. And the concept of time fascinates me. Is time a continuum? What is the link it has with space? What if it was not so much a continuum as it was a circle? If it were to speed up or slow down, would we even notice? Was Einstein correct about his theory of relativity? How can his theory be tested or proven? There are many things I want to know about the way that time works. And maybe someday, I will find a way to test my own various theories.

Brushing. I strongly advocate the use of this technique. I think this may help! This is a process by which a surgical brush is used to stimulate the tactile senses by brushing the arms, legs, and back of the individual. The result for me is a loss of sensory pain for approximately 45 minutes to maybe an hour. It is nice to be able to move without pain. I have considered the possibility of long-term side effects, and it seems to me that those are pretty close to zero. There are only two people in my life who will do this for me at the moment. I really wish there were more. I can feel the difference. And it is pretty drastic. It is an hour of freedom. I wish I could run to someone every hour and have them brush me down, but reality does not seem fit to allow it. Too bad; my life would be much easier. (Obligatory disclaimer: Always consult an occupational therapist before beginning any program like this.)

Auditory Training. This is a therapy developed in France by Dr. Guy Berard. Berard claims that by using his technique, you can possibly fix the auditory problems in the ears. It has been said to greatly reduce the hypersensitivity that many people with autism experience.

The procedure itself is fairly simple. You listen to music through high fidelity headphones twice a day for 10 days, one-half hour per session. Sessions are three to five hours apart. Music is filtered through a device called the audiokinetron. Through this device, the ears are "retrained" to not be quite as sensitive as they were. Exactly how the music is filtered is dependent upon the results of a personal audiogram given before the treatment begins. The audiokinetron is then custom filtered to meet the needs of the individual.

My understanding of auditory training is that in the majority of cases, there has been "some" improvement. Every now and again the auditory training turns out to be the sound of a miracle, but this seems to be rare. Yet most parents I have talked to have been pleased with the results. They notice a clear improvement in the behavior of the child.

I believe one reason this therapy shows promise is because autism is a multi-sensory disorder. The other senses are affected as much as the auditory. And in clearing the problems with the auditory sense, you also to some extent improve the remaining senses. And as interest in sensory integration grows, there appears to be more research being done in this area. I know that the auditory, tactile/proprioceptive, and visual sensory problems can in many cases be treated. Unfortunately, I have seen that one therapy alone usually will not do much to help, but if you experiment with different ideas and different theories (avoid those that can hurt your child), you may eventually stumble onto a combination that shows vast improvement. True, this is not very scientific, but right now it is all we have. I would also say to avoid drugs if at all possible. But should it turn out that drugs can indeed be beneficial, please use the lowest possible dosage. Your child deserves this consideration.

I have included a copy of the Spring 1993 Advocate article on my experience with auditory training in Part Two of this book.

52

Facilitated Communication. At the time of this writing, this is *the* most controversial topic in the field of autism. And it is not without reason. Studies indicate that it does not work. Period. Yet many parents, teachers and advocates swear that it *does* work. Who to believe?

The way this works is the person who wants to communicate is given a computer or a letter board or some other device. Another person holds the hand of the first person, applying gentle pressure in the opposite direction of the device used to communicate. Through a simple pointing or typing procedure, this person is now able to communicate appropriately. Some say this works, while others swear that it is the person who is holding the hand that is doing the communicating, perhaps unknowingly.

I have yet to see any hardcore scientific research that shows F/C to be a valid technique. I have heard rumors that such studies are out there, yet I have not seen them. And I have found it very common for people who do not agree with the results of studies to claim that the research was done incorrectly. (And this goes for the auditory training studies as well.)

At the same time, it is very hard to ignore the growing number of testimonials from those who claim to have had success.

So what is the answer? To believe or *not* to believe? That is the question. And each of us must look at the evidence and make up our own minds. And each of us has a right to those varying opinions.

I believe that one essential key to success, be it in F/C or any other endeavor, must be the capacity to look beyond our own experiences. What is good for the goose is *not* necessarily good for the gander. Just because one form of treatment proves successful for one individual with autism, that does not mean that all will benefit from it.

I must believe that somewhere inside these children are thoughts and feelings (*and intelligence*) that are screaming to be free. If I do not believe this, then I do not deserve to be an advocate. Statistics claim that approximately 70% of the individuals diagnosed with autism have some form of mental retardation. I refuse to believe this. I think that there are those who do, but that number is *far* less than 70%. Some would say that I am just being idealistic. Let them say that. Just because you do not have the ability to talk, this does *not* mean you have nothing to say. And they have just as much of a right to communicate as the rest of us. Whether or not the way they choose to do it is by F/C or not, that will depend on a number of factors. This technique is controversial, and rightfully so. But at the same time, it is far too precious to dismiss entirely.

And even if it goes on to help even just one person communicate, it will be worth it. There are anecdotal stories and cases of those who started out with F/C, and are now typing independently. And just like the auditory training successes, these cases need to be studied, and we need to find the commonalties between them so if at all possible, we can know in advance who will benefit from this technique.

I am in favor of F/C. I think it is a wonderful idea. But I will also be the first to admit it does not work on everyone, and that further research is absolutely necessary to determine once and for all (and to the satisfaction of everyone) if this concept is valid.

Psionic sensors. No, I did not make up that name. It was given to me by an adolescent I once knew who's only goal in life was to somehow acquire autism. (He was interested in the savant abilities.)

There are two theories about where this comes from. People have been trying to prove telepathy in individuals with autism for over 30 years and so far no one has succeeded. Yet some still claim adamantly that it is there, based mainly on anecdotal evidence. Others claim it is simply a matter of reading body language and other "subtleties." Somewhere in the explanation they do mention that somehow people with autism are better at this than the general population.

My personal interpretation is that both are saying *almost* the same thing. Just that one side is saying it in a way that explains it in a way that tends to lend more validity to the concept.

Either way, I have had personal experience along these lines. This started while I was in the hospital and it has been there ever since. It is rare that I know what anyone is actually thinking, but concurrent emotions are very common. If these abilities do in fact exist in many people with autism, it could be considered a rather cruel practical joke of nature. Because it took me a long time (and an ungodly number of mistakes) before I learned how to appropriately react.

Eye contact seems to be the key for me. Almost like there is a sequence written on the eyes of the other person that tells my brain and my emotions exactly how they should be feeling at that point. These feelings are inevitably always what that other person happens to be feeling at the time. And I have noticed that the link is much stronger if I am actually touching the person.

Regardless of whether it is telepathy or a learned body language reading skill, I did not ask for this ability and I do not much care for it. I feel I have more than once invaded domain that was meant to be kept personal. I sometimes still feel guilty about it. But it is not all bad in that I have learned from it.

I have learned that there is much more pain and sadness in the world than there is joy and happiness. And I have learned other things. One night, I was rocking Alesha to sleep. (Melanie's little girl by previous marriage.) She was around a year and a half old at the time. I found her emotions to be very gentle and pure. It was a delight to be able to rock her. And though she was young, she taught me that night that emotions are nothing less than a complex and beautiful language in and of themselves. And like all languages, this language had to be taught. It had to be learned. And Alesha taught me, and I will always be grateful to her for doing so.

Sometimes I wonder if maybe the answer is that this is simply an ability that is acquired by necessity. I know that I needed (and still do need) all the help I can get when it comes to social interaction. Maybe this is actually some kind of talent borne from a simple need for that talent to be there.

Gazing. Along these same lines, I have found that when I am interacting with someone, it helps me to gaze very deeply into their eyes. It gives me more of a *feel* for what they are thinking or feeling, or saying to me. There is a "connection" there that I can sense. And it makes me less afraid of who I am talking to.

I have been told, by those who have noticed I was doing it, that *there is a way to communicate through silence*. And I believe this to be true. And when it is possible for me to do that, I choose to do so if I can. But sometimes this gets me into trouble. When I was working at the Bonded gas station, the manager told me he was "getting complaints" about it, and I was ultimately let go. I guess I am just not cut out for the customer service business.

Those who know about it are not really so much frightened as they are amused. Gazing into friend Brandy's eyes is like removing her body, exposing the soul. This is one reason I love her so much. And I try very hard to build relationships with others like her. The ones who are transparent. For it is those who are not transparent that frighten me. Those who have a closed and narrow mind. Closed to the point that they will not allow anyone in, not allow anyone to get close to them. I greatly fear these people, and I try to avoid them.

Those who look for answers, those who try to understand, those who are willing to hold me, it is those people I spend my time with. And those people that I need to survive. And I know that I am very dependent on them.

Voices. There are "voices." Not really just one voice, but several voices. I can even define some of them for you.

There are voices that sing to me. They do not sing any words or even any particular tune that is discernible to me. But they *do* sing. Not in the standard sense that they sing a song, more of a melody. And that melody always varies. I do not think they have ever sung the same melody twice.

There are voices that scream at me. These are the ones I hate the most. Because they just scream. They come out of nowhere and scream and even give me a headache.

There are voices that tell me to go out and kill people. I ignore them completely.

Then there is the other, last voice. A single voice. A soft voice. A compassionate voice. A knowledgeable voice. A loving voice. A caring voice. A psionic voice. And I know beyond any shadow of a doubt that I would not be functioning without this voice. It speaks to me, calmly and gently. It speaks to me of others. Who they are, how they are, why they are. It tells me when people are not telling me the truth. It tells me when people are not being entirely honest. It tells me the motivation behind that. It tells me how they feel about me and about themselves. It tells me if they've had a rough day. It tells me why. It tells me what they are thinking. It tells me things that they do not want me to know. It tells me when something bad is about to happen and how to avoid it. It makes up 80 to 90 percent of my psionic sensors, but sometimes, it can be hard to tell the difference between this voice and some of the others. I can, but sometimes I have to listen very carefully.

Here is an example:

I was talking to a friend and something strange happened. We were talking to some others, and one of the others said he was hungry. Then she (the friend) said that she had not had anything to eat all day. And when she said that, the voice in my head *immediately* spoke. And it said only one word.

Pregnant...

And so I asked her if she was pregnant again. And she didn't answer me for a minute. And then she said, "Maybe, maybe not." Convinced that the voice does not lie, I pushed her a little. "So which is it? Yes? No? Day late?" She eventually told me (privately) that she was. Then she told me that she had been pregnant six times before, and all of them had ended in miscarriage. (I was there for the sixth one. Not a very pleasant thing to see.) And she told me that I was not allowed to tell anyone, because she was afraid of losing this one. And she did.

Alternate Reality. (A/R) All of a sudden, it came to me. I was just chatting on-line with the modem and I realized all at once that I could describe it. And that the problem was I was not looking to describe anything beyond the darkness, which is the only part that is not describable. But we run into a problem. These two worlds *must* be kept separate. Both are equally real. And if the two of them should start to merge into one in my head (which has happened before), then I have some problems.

There is a darkness. There is no other way to describe it. And you can be surrounded, even, but you are still alone. Kind of like being "alone in a crowd" only much worse. There is only one thing in this darkness, and that would be fear. You are alone and you are scared. And yet sometimes, you *want* to be there. Sometimes the darkness is necessary. What I have always known, but did not realize until recently, is that the darkness is just one small aspect of the rest of the reality.

The darkness lies south. A/R is always entered from the south, because you must get past the darkness to get to the rest of it. (And getting past the darkness can, at times, be very difficult.) Just north of the darkness, over the mountains and facing south, is the castle. The castle is huge and quite majestic. Moats, parapets, you name it, it is all there.

The castle is situated in a valley of sorts. The castle is the only thing in the valley. It is surrounded by mountains on every side of it. The mountains are covered with flowers and trees of all shapes, colors, and sizes. You can walk, run, even roll around on the mountains, all without hurting the flowers. I do not know how you can do this, only that anything is possible within the boundaries of one's own imagination. The best part is that the castle is not deserted. (There is another place which is deserted, maybe I will get to that later.) Kralyn and FireFlyte live there.

FireFlyte is the white winged stallion that you can ride and fly around on. Very friendly, he is, and it is possible to communicate with him, although I cannot describe to you how that is done. He can run with the speed of the huntress cheetah, and he can soar as the eagle soars. I think he is symbolic of the ultimate expression of freedom. Do you want to run away from it all? Hop on FireFlyte's back and soar.

Kralyn is the cute female ... something ... that lives in the castle. She has long, dark, wavy hair that covers her sexy pointed ears, and she has eyes that are as blue as the cloudless sky on a mid-summer's day. And her skin is very lightly coated with white fur. Not much, just enough that she feels like a bear when you hug her. And hug her is all I do. You cannot make love with someone that does not exist. Although I would venture to guess that many people have tried to do just that...

Within the castle (on the top floor) is the library. This is the only place in either reality where you can read poems and other literature that has never been written. The library is quite sizable, taking up the entire third floor of the castle.

There is only love in the valley. There is no sadness, there is no anger, there is no fear, there is no hurt, there is no pain. Only love. And the valley itself resists technology, which makes it all the more enticing. There are no computers, no telephones, no cars, no nothing. Just nature at its finest and its cleanest. It is the ultimate escape, which is why I spend most (but not all) of my time in A/R there. (Exception: Darkness.)

To the east of the valley, and over the mountains (on the way to the city) is the Dragon Field. This is a big field. The kind you would just love to have a picnic in. Only this field has no bugs to annoy you. No ants, no flies, no bees. Just an occasional bird and a butterfly or two. And the field goes on for miles and miles before coming to...

The City. The city, I think, is as close to this reality as the other reality gets. It is covered by this big crystal type of dome, and the way in is that you just walk through. The dome does not open or separate for you, but you still get through it somehow. Then there you are in the city. The city is a very busy place, like most cities are. People are rushing here and there trying to get to places even they do not know about. (Much like the people in this reality, it seems.) All the emotions can be found here, even the negative ones. And things are slightly more technical there then they are at the castle. it is not my favorite place to be, so I tend to spend very little time there.

To the west of the castle (and again, over the mountains) is the ocean. It is a very tranquil place. Very nice to fly over with FireFlyte. Various fish and waterfowl can be found there, and they are all quite friendly. Wouldn't even dream (so to speak) of going fishing here. Ducks and seagulls and dolphins, etc.

The nicest thing about the ocean is that you can breathe in it. The water is a nice lavender color that goes well with the pink sand, giving the whole area a serene feeling about it. The sand is always dry, even when the water comes up, but you can build castles in the sand anyway. The creatures that live in there like to play little hide-and-seek type of games. And my favorite thing to do is dive off of FireFlyte's back, right into the ocean. It is the perfect escape, being a world within another world within another world.

Within the ocean is a sunken boat/ship. I have no idea where it came from, maybe the city. The ship is rather interesting to explore, having all the features you would expect to find, from skeletons to treasure. If you get in the vicinity of the ship (which is about 60 miles or so off the shore), then you can dive through the sand. Down, down, down, keep diving. Do not worry about holding your breath, there is no need. At last you will come to the caverns. The caverns are below the sand, which is below the ocean. When you plow through the bottom of the sand, the top of the cavern kind of "resets" itself. So you would never know you have come through.

The caverns are light. By that I mean that the gravity is quite a bit less than normal. And there is a natural red fluorescence about them. I am not sure where it comes from. You can explore the caverns, which go on for miles. And then when you want to go back to the ocean, you *jump*. The top of the caverns lets you through, and no matter where you jump from, you always end up back by the ship.

To the north and behind the castle (over the mountains) is the forest. Big forest! I think it would take years to explore it all, but there is plenty of reason to explore it.

Within the forest is the abandoned mansion. I think I will keep the details of that to myself, thank you very much.

There is also much terrain I have not even been to yet (and so I do not know what is there). But I am afraid if I check it out, I will go so deep into the A/R that I will not find my way back home. And I want to find my way home.

The only way back home that I know of at the moment is back through the darkness. It is like this darkness is a buffer between one world and the next. I have, in the past, taken others into the darkness with me. But I do not recall ever getting anyone else beyond it. I think it is a solitary venture, and that it needs to be that way. I do not think I myself had much to do with the design of the place, it seemed to be pretty much created for me over the past several years and it continues to evolve. I have talked to a couple others about it, and they say it sounds like a nice place. Perhaps it does. And it is real. Very real. Autistics have the advantage there. The disadvantage is that it can (and does) become so real, that it can get to the point that you do not know which world is which anymore.

Anger. When I was very young, I was quite the violent person. I am not exactly sure what it was. But it was like there were these demons in me. I would go bonkers and run into the bathroom and lock the door so no one could get to me. And then I would sit on the floor and cry as quietly as I could. And while the rest of the family was outside the bathroom, trying to figure out what the hell I just did, and why I did it, I was inside the bathroom, trying to figure out what the hell I just did, and why I did it.

It was like it was not me who was doing it, but someone else who was inside me who was doing it. And I would be watching this person do these things, and I would be aware that he was doing them, but he would not let me in on *why* he was doing them. And I can assure you that as confused as my parents and family were about it, I was far more confused than they were. How I wish someone would have taken the time to tell me what was wrong with me. Would have made it more bearable. But apparently, nobody knew. Eventually, I decided that whoever it was inside was simply not being fair and was not playing by the rules. Fortunately, he is not there anymore, and I am not violent anymore. He still pops up on occasion, but I now know how to keep him pretty much under control.

CHAPTER SIX

"Professionals" and More Ideas on Autism

The professionals of the autism field have responsibilities. For instance, if the child is diagnosed as having autism, the professional should inform the parents the child is autistic, rather than saying he is "developmentally delayed." Too many times I have heard the tragic story that the parents were unaware of the diagnosis, simply because the doctor was not straight with them. Some parents have speculated that maybe the doctor was trying to spare the feelings, but they would rather have gotten the truth. The truth does hurt, but at least it is the truth. And you have to begin somewhere.

Professionals are also obligated to keep current with research and therapies. More than once, I have paid to see a professional and ended up paying to teach them things about autism they already should have known. If your doctor does not seem to know as much about autism as you do, perhaps it is time to see about finding a new doctor.

I have noticed that I tend to not agree with the ideals and philosophies of many of the professionals in the autism field. This is not surprising, though, considering how little is known of the disorder and how many various theories are out there. One thing I have done to deal with this is to work on compiling a list of people that *Thomas* believes to be the best professionals the field of autism has to offer. In the two years that I have been doing this, this list has grown to be all of four people. How I wish it would reach the sky!

The first thing I did was choose criteria for the list. This was very difficult. In order to do this, I looked at what was needed to succeed in working with an individual with autism. This is the criteria I came up with.

1) They must have an understanding of the definition of autism. This does not mean that they have the DSM diagnostic criteria memorized. What is listed does not even scratch the surface of what autism is. No, they must have an understanding that goes deeper than that. They must be aware of the sensory problems, they must have knowledge on how they are treated and how they may be treated in the future. They must understand the subtle reasons for the lack of communication skills, and have an understanding of the intense fear that people with autism often experience.

2) They must know how to act on that understanding of autism. This is, quite frankly, where many of the professionals fall short. I want people who are willing to look at a *person* with autism and see a person. Someone who has value, who can be (must be!) treated with the respect and the dignity that all other people are naturally treated with. Someone who is willing to accept the autism and to be a friend anyway. Someone who is willing to take into consideration the sensory factors and to adjust accordingly. Someone who is able (and willing) to meet the "special needs" of the person with autism in a way that is both friendly and professional.

3) They must be a professional in the field of autism and have no autistic children of their own. (Unfortunately, this excludes several people that would otherwise have a very good chance of going on the list.) Auditory training practitioners also are ineligible for the moment.

4) They must understand Thomas. And while this may in fact be nothing but vanity on my part, I feel that if they can understand me, they can understand anyone.

The four people that I have found who meet the criteria are: Mira Rothenberg, Diane Twachtman, Neatha Lefevre, and Toni Flowers. As a member of the board of directors of the Autism Society of America, I am unable to endorse anyone or anything. But as an individual with autism, I can and *do* endorse these four wonderful people. I have spent many hours with each of them, discussing (in detail) autism and other issues. I am absolutely amazed at the insight they have into autism, having never experienced it themselves. There are several people who are very near being on the list. (And one person is making me want to lift my restriction about auditory training.) I hope to add to this list soon. And I pray that I never have to remove anyone from it.

Diagnosis. I feel the diagnostic criteria for autism needs a major overhaul. At the time of this writing, all we have is autism and pervasive developmental disorder (not otherwise specified), said to be kind of a non-autism type of autism.

First thing we need to do is get rid of the PDD(NOS) diagnosis. Many children who are clearly autistic have been diagnosed PDD. Yet because this diagnosis does not have the word "autism" in it, these children are denied services they need, and that they *should* be entitled to.

It has been said by many advocates and professionals that there are in fact different sub-types of autism. And I believe this. Research needs to be done and these sub-types need to be listed separately. In some cases, it is known that

62

certain forms of therapy show better results with certain types of autism. This information, too, should be made easily available.

Religion. I am not a fan of organized religion. I think it is dangerous to a degree. Yes, I realize that even the Bible commands fellowship, and that we should worship together, but when it gets to the point that the church says who you can and cannot marry, and who you can and cannot divorce, and what movies you can and cannot see, then it has gotten out of hand.

I think that religion, or a faith of any sort, be it Christian, Jewish, Hindu, whatever else is out there, should be a personal thing between the person and their god. And I think that there is room for all of it here in the world. So many people believe that they are so right. That the way they have chosen is the only one and true way. And that if you do not believe as they do, then sometimes they even want nothing to do with you. For example, if I were to believe in the "sacrificial blood of the lamb," anyone else, as far as I am concerned, has every right to believe what they want. We must all, at some point in our lives, choose a path that is right for us. And just because one path is right for me, that does not mean it will be right for everyone else. We are all different. And that is what makes the world so special, and what makes it such a wondrous place to live in.

I believe in a higher being. I am not sure whether or not I believe that this being is "God" in any sense that is commonly regarded as canon, but I believe we were created, and therefore we must have a creator. I also very strongly believe we are not alone in the universe. To be the only planet with life in a universe as big as it is simply does not make any sense to me. I believe that someday, maybe not in my lifetime, but someday we will find signs of intelligent life elsewhere in the universe.

I also believe in the power of prayer. I do not know if it is a psychological power or a spiritual power or maybe both, but I am convinced that there is a power in the art of prayer.

Sensory Integration. Like every other person with autism, I have difficulties in this area. Others have said it and I will say it. It is *frustrating* when your body does not work like it is supposed to.

I think for me the most aggravating problem would be the pressure cravings. If I did not have to put so much of my energy into dealing with this, I could get a lot more done every day.

There is a constant, low-intensity pain going through me at all times. Sometimes it is not so low-intensity. And there are many things that I want to do, many things that I know that I *should* be doing, and sometimes I cannot do these things because I have to put that energy into dealing with this pain. This I find to be very frustrating.

When I was visiting a friend in Vancouver, Washington, I had the opportunity to crawl into one of Temple Grandin's squeeze machines. This was at the Center for the Study of Autism, in Newberg, Oregon. I got in and pulled the lever and there was not enough pressure. I asked Dr. Steve Edelson to increase the pressure, which he did, then there *still* was not enough pressure.

For me, brushing (mentioned on page 56) has a better effect and is more beneficial. Also, since it seems my problems are severe enough that the brushing has no effect if it is done through clothes (something I could never bring myself to tell the occupational therapist who, in reality, was brushing me for very little gain).

Once I realized there was a problem with pressure, I designed a device to help me deal with it. Looks just like a standard watch. But it is much more. And it is remarkably effective, even in it's simplicity. What I have is a waterproof Casio model CA-53W that has been modified with a Speidel wristband. I took the smallest one I could find and knocked another 6 links out of it. The point was to get it as tight as I could and still be safe in doing it.

So now instead of just telling the time, the watch now serves three functions. First, it tells you what time it is as well as doing the calculator and everything else. Second, it provides pressure on the wrist, something I personally have found to be very therapeutic. And third, because of all the buttons and the Speidel, it gives your hands something socially acceptable to do as a release for nervous energy. I have grown very dependent on it the past few years, and I know I would be absolutely lost without it.

I have experimented with creating something to give the other wrist a balance. First I tried a second watch. People asked me what I was doing wearing two watches. I told them I wanted to be twice as sure I knew what time it was. Needless to say, that did not go over too well. I soon abandoned that idea. Then I gutted an old analog watch, leaving nothing but the case. I put a Speidel on it equal to the one on the other wrist. People would ask me why I was wearing it and I would simply say, "This is a watch for people who do not care what time it is."

Unlike the double watch, this has gotten a positive response in the past. Many people have said it is a good idea and that they are going to make one just like it. Maybe I can start a fad.

Another thing I do to deal with the pressure cravings is put on the Pressure Suit. This is a device designed by Michael, Gwendolyn, and myself. It consists of a tight scuba suit and a life jacket. The life jacket goes on under the scuba suit to give it more pressure. The valve on the jacket is located in a way that you can manually adjust the pressure, increasing or decreasing it at any time while it is under the suit. While this does work, it presents it's own problems. First, since the suit does not "breathe," it is easy to get very hot (and quickly uncomfortable). Also, I have noticed that it is generally not a good idea to walk around in public in a scuba suit. The only place I have worn it in public is to a party where some friends of mine were gathered and that was only because they wanted to see it. I have, once or twice, pondered wearing it to the grocery store or something just to see what would happen. My thanks to Michael for the idea, and for donating the suit to Thomas. The low-intensity sensory pain is *gone* while I am wearing it.

In the tactile area, my problems seem to be the exact opposite of what autism is reported to be. This leads me to believe that the sensory problems in autism are those of an extreme, one way or the other.

Where most find touch to be painful, I find it to be very soothing, and even necessary. It provides for me a sense of "sensory equilibrium." I find everything inside to slowly move back into focus. This also presents problems as our contemporary American society has strict rules on touch. And very few people are even willing to acknowledge that platonic affection even exists. So it is often misinterpreted.

Temperature is also a factor. Cold causes severe, physical pain. Heat is soothing, sensory equilibrium. I have heard reports of parents noticing the same thing, and some of them say it is cold the kids like and heat that is troublesome.

Inanimate objects are another matter. There are times when I just can't touch anything because my hands feel like they are on fire if I do. Usually this just applies to certain textures, though I can't tell you which ones because they vary from day to day, hour to hour, minute to minute. It sometimes gets so bad that even the air circulating in the room hurts. Thankfully, this is rare. And I am only effected at the hands and feet. I have heard other cases where the person is effected all over. And I feel for them. As bad as it is for me, it must be very awful or even intolerable for them.

My vision has problems, too. The color yellow is *blinding*. Looking at anything yellow is like looking directly into the sun, even if it is nowhere near as bright.

At the 1993 International Conference in Toronto, I mentioned this in my talk and the response was somewhat overwhelming. One man who was wearing a yellow shirt actually got up and left in the middle of the presentation. Another man who was wearing a yellow button covered it with his hand while he was talking to me, explaining that he did not wish to cause me pain. And while I greatly appreciate these two gentlemen going out of their way for me, it was unnecessary. This is my problem, not theirs, and I must deal with it. Yellow is a very common color, and I cannot dismiss it or avoid it entirely, however much I may want to.

Fluorescent lights bother me, and this has caused a few sensory overload problems at ASA board meetings. Though nothing that can't be worked out. To be in crowded places with people moving in all directions I also have problems with. This includes the conferences. But when things get too rough on me, I just retreat to my hotel room or some other "quiet" place for a while to slow down and get my bearings. Then everything is okay again.

Bright lights are not a good thing. There have been times where I have stepped outside into the sun and (quite literally) gotten sick. Flashing and strobe lights have the same effect, only it is much worse.

As mentioned above, foods are very hard for me. I have heard in most cases, it is a matter of texture. And to some extent, this is true for me as I have noticed that most (if not all) the foods I eat have a very soft texture to them.

But for me it is also a matter of taste. I do not really know how to explain it, other than the fact that most foods simply do not taste good to me. And most taste bad enough that I just can't eat them.

There is a difference between doing things because you want to do them and because you need to do them. The things that I want to do, those things which I have a desire to do, these things I have no problems getting done. But things that I do not really want to do but that need to be done anyway, these are things that hold me back. This has been a problem in school. But sometimes if I am interested enough in the subject, I get deeply involved and actually enjoy it. My civilizations course is an example of this. I found studying the cultures of the ancient Greek and Romans to be fascinating. Comparing the forms of architecture with the attitude and the ways of the culture was also interesting.

However, the physics course was very different. I just couldn't grasp the way it worked. I wanted to, I wanted to understand physics. And when I explained to the teacher (who insisted on calling us all by our last names, perhaps due to a complete lack of respect), he basically told me that if I did not understand, it was pretty much my own fault and there was nothing he could do to help me. Because I did not understand the concepts he was discussing in class, I did not have much of a desire to do the work. Because my interpretation was that I was going to fail anyway. I did not fare too well in that course, and I believe it was after that course that I left college.

I have since taken to getting the occasional physics book out of the library, and I understand physics much better now. No thanks to one bad teacher. But if I need to teach myself to be educated, so be it. That is what I will do.

Temple Grandin has often described problems with wearing certain kinds of clothes. And I have problems here, too. Though mine are completely different from hers.

When I am alone in the condominium, I usually wear a Speedo swimsuit and a heavy sweatshirt. This is what I am most comfortable in. I can't wear shorts, and I haven't worn them since I was about six years old. I prefer long sleeves to the short ones. I am thinking it is a symbolic pressure kind of thing. And I absolutely *hate* business suits. I don't even own one.

Haircuts are *awful* for me. They are very painful and I always wait until the last possible minute (or a conference presentation) to get one. The worst thing would be combs. There are also not many hairbrushes I can use, but there are a few, thankfully.

Bars of soap are a problem. But I have found that I can use liquid soap. This is more expensive, but it doesn't hurt as much so it is well worth the extra cost to me. I have problems with a lot of shampoos, too. The one I like the best is Vidal Sassoon Ultra Care. Razors are a nightmare. But I have found that rotary razors are tolerable. Anything else, I just can't use.

Therapies and Methodologies. There have been several methods of treatment used on me over the years. I would like to discuss what they were, what worked, what did not, and *why*. First, this is what did not do any good:

When I was very young, my parents believed strongly in paddling their children when they did something wrong. For me, this was ineffective. One

67

example (out of many) that I can give is the very vivid memories of being paddled *every* Sunday after church.

If they had to go through this every Sunday, it was obviously not doing what it was supposed to. In addition, it made me greatly fear going to church because I knew what would happen to me when we got home. This was family tradition. Very few (if any) of us four kids *wanted* to wake up on Sunday mornings to go to church. But our parents wanted to teach us about God. They wanted us to respect Him. They wanted us to love Him. What they were doing in my case is accomplishing the exact opposite. The Bible clearly states that, *"Fear of the Lord is the beginning of Wisdom."* If this is true, then I was profoundly wise when I was a child.

I had no idea what I was doing wrong. And they never *told* me in a way I could understand. So the paddling simply turned out to be abuse in my mind, and that process created a lack of trust which still exists to this day.

There was a very similar incident that occurred when I was in the seventh grade. My health class took a field trip to the science museum here in Columbus. We were warned that anyone who left the group would be paddled. I left the group. Not because I wanted to, but because the sensory overload demanded it. I wanted to stay with the group desperately, but I was simply unable to do so. I needed to find a place that was a little more quiet and less stimulating to calm down. Afterward, I rejoined the group on my own. I didn't think anyone even missed me.

The trip was on a Friday. And the following Monday, I was requested to report to the office. I walked in to find a little over half my health class, who quickly informed me they were doing a paddling assembly line type of thing. One of us right after the other went into the principal's office to get our just desserts.

Then it was my turn. I went in and the principal and health teacher gave me a long (and boring) lecture on why I was there and what they were going to do to me. They asked me to lean on the chair and then the health teacher asked me if I had any back problems.

My response: "Not yet."

I suspect I probably got it worse than anyone else for saying that.

During my entire childhood, I was going to doctors, psychologists and psychiatrists. No one knew what was wrong, and they all did the same tests on me over and over. I can't even begin to count the number of times I have had to put the round peg in the square hole.

This did not help me. What it did was leave me angry, frustrated, and more untrusting of the next doctor who came along. I did not want to go through all that *same* testing again. But I always did. And of course, I had no say in the matter. (But one thing that did always help me was when the doctor was also willing to do the same test. I figured if *they* could embarrass themselves, well then so could I.)

They also tried several things in the hospital. For instance, they once initiated this "program" for me whereby I was not allowed *any* physical contact whatsoever. If I were to hug a fellow patient or nurse, or if I were to hold their hand, then I would be *locked* in my room for a period of fifteen minutes as punishment for doing so. To this day, I feel this is one of the cruelest things ever done to me by anyone.

The way we spent our days was to go to various "activities." These were chosen from a wide assortment of activities available, though we, the adolescent patients, rarely got any say in what activities we went to. The decision was made always by the doctor and the team.

One activity that I had in the afternoon was that I would walk to this building and get some clay and they would tell me to continuously throw the clay down on a mat, pick it up, and throw it down again. While this was going on, I would at the same time be talking to a therapist about whatever it was that was bothering me that particular day.

I must say that I never saw the reason why I needed to do this. If someone wanted to talk to me, there was a way he would have gotten much more out of me than by this method they used. What they should have done was take me away from everyone else in the room who was doing it to a quiet room and sit down and just *talk*. There was no need to play that silly clay game, and I could have done without the sensory overload it caused me. My tactile senses did not like the way the clay felt, my auditory senses did not like the sound it made when it hit the mat on the table, and my visual senses did not like the random movement of everyone else in the room. If I *did* feel like talking to him, then I would eventually start talking and stop throwing the clay. But he would not let me talk to him unless I was throwing the clay. So every time he was about to get something from me, he ruined it by interrupting to insist I throw the clay. I usually stopped talking at that point because it became obvious to me that he could really care less about what I had to say or how I felt. This therapist was more interested in the clay than he was in me.

Just outside the room where the clay was, there was an area where the patients sawed logs. If they were not sawing logs, they were chopping those logs with an axe. These logs were eventually picked up to be used as firewood. The patients got no compensation for the work they did to prepare the logs. (Slave labor by any other name would smell just as foul.) I was "assigned" to this activity for a time. It was here that I learned of the physical pain of manual labor. Not the kind of pain you usually have when you work out or do something strenuous, that I can handle. This went far beyond that. I do not know if it was because of underdeveloped muscles or because of an autistic proprioceptive system, or because of some combination of both. What I do know is that these people were hurting me. And they didn't seem to care.

A lot of the psycho-therapies I feel were ineffective. Many of them focused on some form of group therapy where you would receive criticism and feedback about the way others perceived you. At other times, you would be in the basement offices with the doctor(s) discussing the way you "felt" at that particular moment.

While anyone can see the benefits of either or both of these forms of therapy, they are not what I needed at the time. I would eventually need them, but I needed something else first. And that something else is what they failed to give me.

There was no need for them to ask me how I felt. The answer should have been obvious. I felt *confused, frustrated,* and *scared to death.* And that is all I felt. It was really just that simple. I was confused because I had no idea what was wrong with me and why I had these problems I did, and I was frustrated because I did not know what to do about them or how to fix them. And I was scared because, well, because I was *always* scared.

What I needed was for someone to sit down with me and say, *"Look, Thomas, this is what the problem is. This is what it is called, this is what it means, this is why your ears hurt, this is why you need to be held, this is why you see things differently than the rest of us, this is why you can't eat, this is why you can't do the schoolwork, this is why you don't understand the math, this is why you can write and play music better than the rest of us, this is why you retreat into your own world, this is why people frighten you, and this is what we can do to help you with it."*

What is so difficult about that? Why did they not do it? Having that explained to me, I would have at least known what it was I was fighting. And you can't fight something without knowing what it is.

70

Sometimes, someone would come up with an idea that did have a positive effect on me, even if it was accidental:

When I was growing up, I was raised on songs and stories. There was a constant playing of Irish music in the house. This was very good because it taught me two very important things. And they are things that I have been able to put into this book and into the advocacy, and things that I have been able to take to the ASA board meetings.

I learned of the joys of love, and the horrors of war.

And even when the talks and screaming and reprimands could not get through to me, the music (and the lyrics) did. This was the one connection I had with my mother, who was so deeply in love with Irish music and the Irish culture. The culture did not interest me much. And if I did have questions about it, those questions were always answered in the music.

Unfortunately, her love for the music has since been replaced by her even bigger love for sports, so we no longer have even that connection. And those many records that used to so constantly fill the house with melody, voices, and happiness now lie dormant in the corner, collecting dust and dreaming of days when they again might do heroic things.

But this is an example of something that *did* work for me. Though at the time, none of us knew it was having an effect.

I have always had an interest in electronics. I think this originally came from my strong need to know how the world (and the rest of the universe) works. So I developed this habit of tearing things apart. Occasionally, my father would come home with something from work and I would tear into it or we both would.

And after totally destroying God only knows how many gadgets, I began to learn not only how to take them apart, but how to put them back together. And then when that got boring I learned how to put them back together with more features than they had when I took them apart. This was all self taught by trial and error. I certainly did get "zapped" more than my share of times along the way!

If I had not been allowed to lose so many tools and to ruin so many toys, I would not have the knowledge that I have now that has served me so well. I needed to be able to learn in my own way at my own pace. The rest was easy.

For a while, I was going to an occupational therapist every Monday from 10:00 a.m. to 11:00 a.m.. This is something else that worked. Sensory integration exercises left me feeling very whole and complete. I wish I could go back again. I have lost the feeling of whole and complete since I have left.

I think the thing that has helped me more than anything else, any drug or any form of therapy or any behavior management, is the gentle embrace of a friend. I'm not going to say anything else about it, because there is nothing else about it that needs to be said.

And finally, the last thing that has been most helpful to me would have to be the *Autism Society of America*, for obvious reasons.

P a r t II

Poetry...Writings...Ideas

&

The Future

Do not ask questions. Poetry is just that way. How we see ourselves.

Thomas A. McKean

Gwendolyn

The first time I saw her was at a prayer meeting at Parkland College in Urbana, Illinois. It was the autumn of 1983 and Michael introduced me to her. Or so the story goes. The truth is that I do not remember that. I remember the prayer meeting, and Michael holding out his hand out to me, and I clearly remember the sheer terror I felt the entire time I was there and that Michael, though unaware of the origins of that terror, was aware of the terror itself. But I do not remember the introduction to Gwen. For all I know, one of my best friends is someone I have never officially "met."

The first time I remember seeing her was in the lobby of the school. There was an area where the Parkland Christian Fellowship hung out. I was there talking to some people I knew and Gwen came up with one of those hand held tape recorders with a speaker. She asked me if I wanted to hear a particular song she had been listening to.

Why was this beautiful person wasting her time with me? I wasn't worth her bother! That is how I felt. Yet at the same time, I certainly was not going to push her away. I smiled and told her to play the song. The auditory dysfunction in my ears made it impossible for me to hear it. If I could remember what the song was, I'd ask her to play it again.

I have since asked her why she put all of her effort into forming a friendship with me. Most of the effort was not mine. She went out of her way to become my friend. And no one had ever really done that before. I was completely baffled by this atypical human behavior. Yet I was also intrigued. Could it be that I was finally to know what it would be like to have a *friend*? This is something I had wanted to know for all my life!

She has explained it to me, though not in any way that I truly comprehend. If you were to ask her anything about her beliefs or personality traits, she would invariably link it to some aspect or part of her childhood. Gwen is very much in tune with who she is. And who she was before she became who she is. Her answer to the above question goes back many years. Though I am still not completely sure of what that answer is, I know that she felt a need to be my friend. She knew there was something wrong somewhere, and to make me feel a little better was something she felt she could do, something she felt she needed to do. How fortunate I was! Ten years later, she claims that God had an unseen, if not large part in bringing us together. Considering the friendship that resulted, I find I am unable to find a valid argument against those claims.

It was not before winter followed autumn. And we, the students at Parkland College, faced another typical Urbana, snow bound winter. I did not have a car. I was going to take the '67 Mustang to Illinois with me, but it had been totaled in the accident not long before I left for college. Gwen had a car and she often invited me to go places with her after school. I did not ask her, at least not most of the time. It seemed to be something she *wanted* to do.

My emotions were so torn over this person. Part of me felt so excited and so ecstatic to have such a wonderful and beautiful friend. Yet that other part of me was always seriously trying to figure out, to no avail, what the motivation behind that friendship was.

Gwen was (and remains) a very spiritual person. She does nothing to hide her deep love for, or her deep faith in God or Christ. She reads the Bible in a way that can truly only be described as "religious." She has a very strict code, a strict set of simple guidelines that she lives by. If any action she must take violates these guidelines, she searches long and hard for an alternative action that more closely fits her own very high ethical standards. She is the most moral person I know. And even ten years ago, when we were both much younger and I was lost in another world, I could still see this about her. Because she did everything she could and everything she needed to in order to show me this part of her. And if that involved coming into my own world with me, then she was willing to do that. She very gently and peacefully came into my world and showed me what love really is and what love really means. And I felt very obligated after that to find a way to visit her world since she had so kindly and unselfishly voluntarily visited mine. Something that none of the professionals who had worked with me over the years had ever thought to do.

Another thing that I noticed about her right away was the fact that while she had a deep belief in God, she did not force this belief on others. And this was strange to me. Because many who consider themselves to be a "Christian" also believes in pushing that religion as hard as they can on others. The ones I had met up to that point did, anyway. And if you did not believe *exactly* as they did, they ultimately wanted nothing to do with you. And then all of a sudden here is someone who is totally different. She was somehow able to cast off all the spiritual corruption that had taken place over the centuries, and had been able to go back to the very fundamentals that originally made Christianity the wonderful concept that it is. She loved you. This is what Christ commanded. She loved you as He would love you. She loved you whether you believed as she did or not. Because it was not so much her duty as much as it was her privilege as a Christian to do so. Many people speak of a love of God. Gwen is one of the very precious few who goes so far as to live a love of God. And that may well be what ultimately attracted me to her.

76

I soon found that I could trust her completely. I have copies of literally over 1,000 pages of letters that I have sent her over the past ten years. Many of them have perfect descriptions of autism in them, though I had no idea at the time that describing autism is what I was doing. I was just complaining to someone who would listen about the sensory problems I noticed were there, and I was asking (both her and myself) if it was "normal." The only thing I can recall reading about autism in my mental health classes was that most people with autism are mentally retarded and that it effects communication and social interaction skills.

It was mainly through this mail that I finally found Thomas. And I took some wrong turns along the way (like exploring schizophrenia). I could say whatever I wanted to, I could write and I could *be* as autistic as I wanted to, or needed to be in order to find the answers I was looking for. And regardless of how weird or strange or just bizarre it became, she loved me anyway.

I guess what I am trying to say here is that she has this wonderful ability, and did even back then, to separate the autism from the person inside, and to see only the person. This is something I have noticed very few people can do.

If you were to ask her what autism is, she probably would not be able to give you a good definition. Yet at the same time she has a profound understanding of it that has made my life much easier, and much more fulfilling over the years.

Thank you, Gwendolyn.

An Inside Look At Auditory Training

I will always remember the first time I ever talked to Temple Grandin. This was before I wrote the Mira Trilogy, before I joined the Board of Directors, before I "got involved." I got her number from an old Advocate someone gave me, and she was returning my call. This was around 11:00 p.m., and the conversation was a total disaster. The fault for this was certainly mine, and Temple (who has since become a friend) has told me she remembers nothing of the conversation. Needless to say, I smiled when she said that, and did nothing to jog her memory.

But in the chaos that was the conversation, she gave me some advice. It is advice that is as old as the hills. But I think it still applies today, especially to those of us who write and speak regularly. She said, "All you can do is call them like you see them." And that is what I am going to do in this article. I recently went to Cincinnati, to "Comprehensive Concepts in Speech and Hearing," to have auditory training. I would like to recount my experience with you now.

This all came about late in 1991 when I received mail from Tina Veale, in Cincinnati. She had just set up the auditory training, and had read my article in the state of Ohio ASA newsletter about the auditory dysfunction. She wrote asking me for more information on my adaptive devices.

I have a very strict policy about calling the people who write to me. I believe very strongly that if someone takes the time to write to me, I should take the time to respond in some form. During that conversation, I was invited to hear her speak to the Northwest Ohio chapter in Toledo. I rounded up two friends and pathetically begged them to come with me (my own car was not up to such a trip at that time).

The three of us had front row seats. And as I sat there listening to Tina explain the process and the theory behind it, a little (very little) of my skepticism melted. After her presentation, she asked me what I thought of the process. I told her flat out that the only way she was going to get me to believe in it was to put the headphones on me and prove it. She immediately told me she was willing to do just that.

Considering the cost of auditory training, and considering the fact that my ears are quite sensitive, I would have been a fool to turn down that offer. But I turned it down anyway. My perception of auditory training was, "Here, wear my magic headphones for 10 hours, and I will fix your ears." See, I grew up in a home with the world's most skeptical parents. And I guess a little rubbed off on me because I didn't buy it.

As I became more involved with the ASA, I continued to read more about auditory training. I looked for bad things, but I couldn't find any. Articles and letters claimed kids had been helped. Parents told me it made all the difference. Then, at the conference in Albuquerque, Annabel Stehli finally talked me into it. I made an appointment with Tina. I went in somewhat reluctantly, but with an open mind.

The office was quite a bit smaller than what I had imagined it would be. I guess this is because I had seen a video of someone getting auditory training, and it was a child sitting in this big room. He was wearing the headphones and he was sitting on this mat in the middle of a floor. There were tons of toys all around him, and he seemed quite happy to engage himself with one toy in particular.

But Tina's place was not like that. In fact, the training was in a very small room. There were two little "cubbies" in the room, they were across from each other. There was one machine for each cubby. One was the French model, one was American. The idea was to be able to do two people at once. I observed through the two weeks that most of the kids seemed to either sleep or played with some small toy to keep their interest.

First came the initial audiogram. I was told I would need a hearing aid at some point, because I had significant hearing loss. I said, "I know, ten percent in the right ear." To which she replied, "No, it is much more than that." This led me to speculate that my hearing has gotten worse since the operation on my eardrum in the 70's. I did, at one point, mention the hearing aid to my mother, just in passing. She told me not to worry about it because "every audiogram shows that you are going deaf." But I have decided not to be surprised if it came down to a hearing aid someday very soon.

Later that afternoon, I had my first "session." I walked into the room, sat down in the little cubby. They said they were going to raise the volume and to tell them when it was getting a little loud, which I did. I grew a little excited at this point. One of my main questions about auditory training was what kind of music they played. It was reggae music. I had not heard much reggae up to that point, and I decided to sit back and enjoy a true cultural experience. Mixed in with the reggae was some 15 year-old Stevie Wonder, and even Bob Dylan's Greatest Hits album, which I am very familiar with, having studied his music for several years. They explained to me that there were five or six CD's in the player, and that one song was selected at random from each CD, which in total made up the half hour of music. Usually, it was closer to 25 minutes, which suited me just fine.

The music itself was filtered true to form, at 4000 and 8000 hertz. To me, it sounded like cymbals placed at random locations within the music. You would be chugging along with the tune, and all of a sudden, you would hear a distortion that sounded somewhat like a "clash" and then you were back to where you were. I found the "clashes" to be a bit painful in the ears, while the rest of the time it was quite pleasant. More pleasant than usual, in fact. This process was repeated for ten days. Twice a day for 1/2 hour, four hours apart.

Somewhere into the middle of the first week, I began to notice some changes. The best example of this is the fact that the hotel door had an awful squeal to it when it was opened. At first, this bothered me greatly. But as time passed and as I continued the training, the squeal grew less and less annoying. This caused me to go into training and ponder the ninth chapter of Acts of the Apostles while I was listening. Paul completely changed his mind in light (so to speak) of the new evidence that was facing him. It looked like I might have to do the same. Paul was all too happy to change his mind. It was beginning to look like the same would happen for me.

However well this worked for me, there were still some things about it that I did not like. For instance, the music stayed the same for the duration of the two weeks. They explained that out of 500 some CD's tested, they had found only 30 or so that were qualified for auditory training. Six of those thirty were in the CD player. And while it is certainly not mandatory to change the CD's, I feel that different music would make the process not only more tolerable, but also more enjoyable.

There were also a few times that I felt a bit "talked down to" by one of the staff. I don't think she meant to do this, it may have just kind of "happened." Please allow me to insert a gentle reminder here for everyone reading this. I say this every time I speak, and almost every time I talk to individual parents. And I repeat it here again because I feel it is that important. These children, despite what the statistics say, do have intelligence! They know when they are being patronized, they know when you are talking about them behind their back. Please, please treat them with the respect and the dignity that you would with anyone else. They deserve this. And I feel that you will also see some improvement. Those of you who work with the autistic population, please watch yourselves. Very few things hurt us as badly as others thinking we are aliens or babies. We are not. We are people. Flesh and blood with thoughts and feelings. Feelings which can be, and are, easily hurt. I see this happen so often in my travels. It is not intentional on the part of the people doing it, just as it was not intentional in Cincinnati. But it does happen. And it needs to stop.

The device used in the training was the audiokinetron. The Berard device. I was very fascinated by the technical aspects of how both the audiokinetron and the BGC worked. Later, when I had the pleasure of visiting Dr. Edelson, he let me play with both of them. My thanks to Dr. Edelson for allowing me to do this. It answered many questions for me.

When I left Cincinnati to return to Columbus, my hearing had definitely changed for the better. I noticed I could turn the stereo in my car up a little louder than before. (And I did, when "Rock & Roll Heaven" came onto the oldies station.) The sirens that go by my apartment on the OSU campus did not bother me as much as they used to. For now, instead of hurting, all they did was wake me up in the middle of the night. And I am assuming they do that for everyone. Doors closing, dogs barking, babies crying, people talking to me on the phone, all these things were pain free for the first time in many, many years. I stopped carrying the earplugs around with me, and I began to wonder if all that work I put into rewiring my telephone was really worth it.

(Side note: When I told Temple (during that same first call mentioned above) about my phone modification, she told me I was not the first to think of it. But since I was the first to publish it, it seems I am getting all the credit. This modification greatly reduces the pain from hypersensitivity when talking on the phone. If anyone wants a copy of my schematic, send a SASE to me at the address below. I will send it out to you.)

Tina was very dedicated. She sold her home and moved herself and her family into a smaller one, just so she could afford the Audiokinetron, the BGC, and the training from Berard. It seemed to have worked in my case. Just like she said it would.

A couple of months later, my parents went to their cabin in Tennessee. They asked me to stay at the house and look after things while they were gone. Standard procedure. I was putting the dishes away in the cupboard. I put the plates down on the shelf. The pain was almost unbearable. What happened? I thought I was over this! I walked over to the dishwasher, got some more plates and put them on the shelf, thinking it really didn't happen. It happened again. I stood quietly, looking at that monster that was the rest of the dishes. They looked back at me as if laughing at me in a merciless, malicious fashion. They looked back as if they knew they had won. I realized then that if I were the dishes, I would have done the same thing. I wondered why I had not thought to bring the ear protection I had always brought before. I finished the dishes. Very slowly.

Later that night, the dogs started barking. That bothered me. I had to turn the TV down while I was watching "Nick At Nite." (Preserving Our Precious Television Heritage.) I longed for the modified phone until I got back to my apartment. It is like I blinked my eyes, and had never gone to Cincinnati.

Annabel Stehli informs me that sometimes there is not much noticeable difference in the third to sixth month. If this is true, then I have two more months of this ahead of me. Not a very pleasant thing to look forward to. I am hoping it will settle down again, but only time will tell. I long for the freedom that Tina once gave me. They say you can't miss what you never had. It has been many years since my ears have been normal, until now. I had forgotten what a pleasant experience it was to be able to hear like everyone else. I do not know what caused it to go back to where it was, perhaps it was just meant to be. Auditory training works, but like all things, it does not work for everyone.

One thing I feel obligated to do as a board member is thoroughly investigate EVERY type of treatment available for autism. I feel that I need to do this to be better informed so as to make myself a more valuable asset to the board and on the lecture circuit. (Not to mention to find more answers to my own questions.) I now feel I have looked at auditory training from every angle. Below is a list of questions to ask auditory training practitioners, based on this research, and from talking extensively to the people listed below.

1. Were they trained to do auditory training? Who trained them? Were they trained by Berard or a Berard certified trainer? If they were NOT trained by either of these, don't even bother asking the rest of the questions. Hang up the phone and try someone else. If they say they were trained by Berard and you are still suspicious, ask to see the certificate.

2. Do they do anything at all different from what Berard suggests? If so, what is the reason? Why do they feel their way is better? You will have to use your own judgment in this case, but the closer they are to Berard's original method, the better your results will be.

3. Ask for references. Ask for both professional references and also ask for the phone numbers of at least three people who have gone through the training with this person. Call all references. If they are unwilling to give references, look for someone who has nothing to hide.

4. What do they charge for Auditory Training? If they charge much over $1,000.00, chances are you can get a much better deal somewhere else.

5. Are they willing to come to you? There are some people who are willing to come to your town if a certain amount of people request it. Be careful, because a lot of people charge extra for this.

6. How are the children occupied during training? They should not be allowed to read or to sleep. They should be alert and doing something that causes them to listen to the music.

7. What kind of music is used? Is the music changed at any time during the training? My research shows that the best music to use is reggae, Mozart, or something else with a beat that covers all frequencies.. Berard strongly suggests that the music be picked at random for each session. Some people have the same CD's on the entire time, others refuse to play the same thing twice during the ten days. Either way, make sure that the music they use is on Berard's list.

8. Do they do audiograms? Some people feel they are unimportant. The reality is they are the MOST important part of the procedure. Make sure that three (3) audiograms are included in the deal. Also make sure they are done by a certified audiologist.

9. How open are they about the training? They should be willing to tell you everything they are doing. Ask to have the audiogram explained to you. Ask them where they are filtering the music, and where they are setting the volume. Finally, ask to hear a sample of what your child will be hearing, or to sit in on a session with your child. Also inquire about aftercare.

10. Add your own questions here. I am sure I forgot a few.

Finally, I am sending all three of my audiograms to be published with this article. All three were done at various stages of the training. The first was done on October 5, 1992, before I started, the second on October 9, which was halfway through, and the third on October 16, after I had finished. These don't lie. Good or bad, you be the judge. (See following charts.)

I do not know what else to say, except to publicly thank Tina for the training. (Thanks, Tina. And thanks for the counseling in the office.) She wanted to prove to me that auditory training was valid, and she succeeded. I am now convinced that auditory training does indeed have beneficial effects for many individuals. It is NOT an experience I wish to repeat, but the end results may justify the means if the procedure is done correctly. If anyone has any specific questions, please feel free to write or call me. I will be happy to answer them.

This was originally published in the 1993 ASA Advocate. Of all I have published, nothing has gotten more of a response.

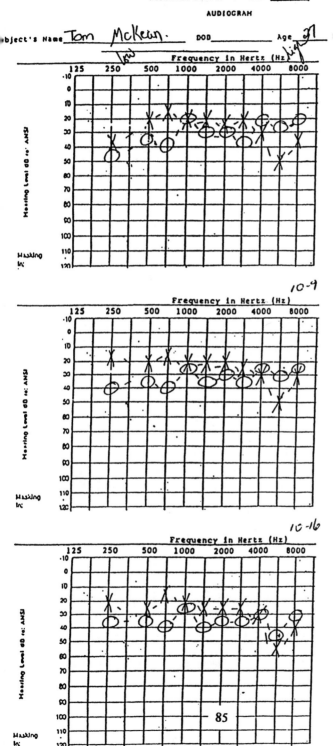

Subject's Name Tom McKean.　　　DOB_____　　Age 37　Date Seen 10-5-92

10-9

10-16

85

X left
O right

The audiogram from 10-5-92 shows a common concern with people with auditory problems, the two ears do not hear at the same level. You will note that Tom's hearing has a large gap from 750 to 1,000 and 3,500 to 4,000 in his right ear and 6,000 to 8,000 in his left ear. Also, there is a large gap between his right ear and left ear at 6,000 Hz. The chart from 10-16-92 shows these gaps all decreasing.

Ms. Tina Veale of Comprehensive Concepts stated that Tom's results, although they show improvement, are less than usual because of his hearing loss problem.

Serenading The Stress

Stress; what is it, and where does it come from? what causes stress, and what are the results? Most importantly, how do we deal with stress?

Stress has been defined in many ways. Selye, founder of   stress research, defines stress as a "stimulus event of sufficient severity to produce disequilibrium in the homeostatic physiological systems." Stress has also been defined as a "nonspecific to the body to any demand that exceeds the person's ability to cope," and as a "person-environment relationship that threatens or taxes personal resources." Stress has even been described as a "mental state in response to strains or daily hassles (Strecker 26)." I personally believe that stress can be best defined as "getting out of bed in the morning."

Robert A. Jud, president of Robert A. Jud and associates, a company offering consulting services in a broad range of adult learning areas as they relate to organizational life, sees seven areas that cause stress in our lives (Strecker 29-31).

1) Change: Change is inevitable. It is as the tide sweeping over the sands of the calm. And while some changes can be positive, such as Christmas, a vacation, or perhaps a promotion to a new and higher paying job, even these things have been known to cause stress.

2) Expectations: The expectations others put on us day to day, as well as the expectations we put upon ourselves, can surely be a cause of stress.

3) Perfectionism: People who overwork themselves to achieve perfectionism may well have a high level of stress, as perfectionism is not at all easy to achieve.

4) Inability to set limits: More and more, as our society increases in speed and pace, I have seen people develop an inability to set limits, until finally, they just "burn out." I have seen this cause stress in many lives, and I have organized my own life accordingly.

5) Conflict and confrontation: I use the classic example here of getting a traffic ticket. For who among us has not felt some form of stress when we

have heard those ominous words, "May I see your license and registration, please?"

6) Type "A" behavior: Those people who are constantly striving for achievement, love, power, (money?), for those people, life can a struggle. The need they feel to get so much done in so little time can be a great cause of stress.

7) Fear of ambiguity: What lies ahead for us as a people? What kind of world are we shaping for our children? Certainly we are faced with stressful situations just by living in this day and age. What with the threat of the nuclear bomb, AIDS, and even the second coming, we feel stress just by being in this environment. Technology has brought the world into our living room. And it is a big world. And it is not nice.

8) Need to be accepted. This is not to be included in the other seven, as I have only just now thought of it. But I do feel that the need to be loved and accepted, by our friends, family, spouse, and coworkers, can be a big cause of stress. This is where the problem of peer pressure comes in, one of the biggest causes of stress for teens today.

The effects of stress vary from individual to individual, as does the ability to cope with stress. Where as some of us can routinely go about our stress filled lives day after day, others of us soon reach the point of no return, and slip into that nervous breakdown that the doctor warned us was coming. Activities such as family get-togethers, children leaving home, retirement, and the spouse beginning or ending work, can all cause stress in our lives. So can other routine inconveniences, such as trouble with the boss, mortgage, and/or divorce. Death of a spouse generally causes the most stress in our lives, where as minor violations of the law, while causing stress, rate very low on the Stress scale (Holmes 71).

What are the effects of stress? Some of us get migraines (My father alone may well be turning a profit for Advil). Some of us just get ill, with sicknesses such as a cold, flu, or other virus.

Blurred vision, sweating, muscle tension, mood shifts, and breathing difficulties can all be signs of stress. Changes occurring in the body might be; elevated blood pressure or elevated blood sugar, a strain on the heart, dilated pupils, or an elevated cholesterol count (Honig 150).

This being the case, it can, and usually does, cause observable behavioral symptoms. When one is feeling stressed, you may notice it by looking for these tell tale signs. Crying, yelling, lack of concentration, depression, anger, frustration, and/or undefined sexual problems (Honig 171).

What are the effective ways of dealing with stress? How can we calm ourselves in these situations? The following are ways that my research, as well as my life, have shown are effective ways of dealing with stress. While these techniques do not work for everyone, they are generally accepted as valid.

1) Set limits: Be reasonable with yourself. Set your goals high, but not so high that you cannot reach them. Try to lose five pounds before losing ten. Try getting a B before going for the A. Take it one step at a time.

2) Time management: I believe this to be the most important and effective way of dealing with stress. Pace yourself. Give yourself time to do those little yet important things, such as walking the dog, or sending that friend a card on her birthday. Assess your priorities, plan a schedule, then stick to it! Knowing where you are going, and having your day planned in advance can reduce stress.

3) Flight mechanisms: Take a warm bath, talk to a good friend, walk in the park, and take the time to stop and smell the flowers. In short, relax. Try to get the problem out of your mind temporarily. You will have time to deal with it later, and you may be thinking more rationally when you do (Strecker 31).

4) Exercise: Exercise can be a good way to relieve stress. A regular regimen of exercise practiced daily, such as sit ups, or push ups, and various aerobics, can drastically cut down on stress.

Yes, stress is a part of life. It fills our days and brings terror to our nights. Yet without it, we would not be human. And by using some common sense techniques, we can control it. Stress is hard to beat at times, but I believe we can beat it. It does not need to have control over our lives.

Works Cited:

Holmes, Thomas H, and T. Stephenson Holmes, MD. "How change can make us ill." Stress. Chicago, Illinois. Blue Cross Association, 1974.

Honig, Alice Sterling. "Stress and coping in children (part I). "Young Children. May 1986: 147-160.

Honig, Alice Sterling. "Stress and coping in children (Part II)."Young Children. July 1986: 161-174.

Luce, Gay G, and Erik Peper. "Learning how to relax." Stress. Chicago, Illinois. Blue Cross Association, 1974.

Strecker, Susan. "Straight talk about stress." The Executive Female. March/April 1985: 26-32.

Note: This is an essay I wrote for college. It got an "A"

How To Buy A Bear

I am very much of the opinion, having slept with a bear myself for a number of years, that everyone, not just babies and children, but everyone should sleep with a bear.

The benefits to your mental health are immeasurable. If you sleep alone, a bear is almost a necessity, and even if you are married (or perhaps sleeping with a significant other), the bear should always be within an easy arm's reach of where you are sleeping. A bear can make you feel less lonely, can keep you warm on cold nights, and if you are talking on the telephone, holding the bear during your conversation can be very nice.

But bears are not as simple as what they would first appear to be. Many bears on the market today fail to take into consideration the needs of the adult population. They are aimed mainly at the parents or friends of parents who are purchasing the bear for their newborn baby. As infants, the kind of bear may not be as important. But as adults, there are ten certain criteria that must be met to ensure the appropriate bear is used. We will be discussing these ten criteria and other related items in this essay. Please keep these items in mind as you go bear shopping.

1) First and foremost; the bear must not be bought by the person who will be using it. This is very important, as it defeats the purpose of the bear. The bear must be given to you by a friend. Not a family member, fiancé or a lover, but a friend. Preferably a friend of the opposite sex, but any friend will do. Keep in mind that there is absolutely zero magic in a bear that you buy for yourself, and magic is what you are looking for. If someone gives you a bear, it is only because they love you. There is much comfort in this thought as you hold your bear. Naturally, it would be best if you did not need to ask for a bear, but many people are unaware of the benefits a bear can offer. So asking a friend to buy you a bear is perfectly acceptable. If you know someone who is an accomplished tailor or seamstress, perhaps you can talk them into creating a bear to order of specifications. Maybe as a birthday or Christmas present. This, then, would be the ultimate bear. For there is even more love in a bear that was made just for you.

2) Size is very important. Due to the high cost of animals, many people who buy bears for friends buy the small bears, simply because they are less expensive. Do not do this. There simply is not enough of the small bears to

hold. Conversely, the larger bears are also a problem. I have found that bears that are seventeen to twenty inches in height are an ideal size. While these bears may run much higher in cost than the others, they may well be worth it. When it comes to bears, you get what you pay for. (The exceptions to this are the giant bears that can run over $100.00 or even more. These are nice on certain occasions, but they should always be homemade.)

3) Consider the fluffiness of the bear. Bears should not be filled too tightly. There should be enough room left in the bear that it can be held very tightly and be squeezed out of shape. Be sure you buy a bear that moves back into its previous shape immediately after the person lets go.

4) Look at the eyes and nose of the bear. Many bears have eyes and noses that could potentially fall off of the bear. Make sure that the bear you buy (or have) has eyes and noses that are securely on the bear. Due to parental demand, companies have gotten better about this.

5) The ears of the bear are also very important, and serve a necessary and useful purpose. Ears are very good to nibble when you are alone or depressed. Not so much in such a way that the ears get wet, just a gentle nibble will do fine. The best ears for nibbling on a bear are the kind that stick up in the air. Floppy ears are not good on a bear, and should be avoided. Also, the ears should be placed not only on the top of the head, but also toward the back of the bear. It is okay if they are in the middle of the top, but ears that are more toward the back are easier to access for nibbling.

6) The arms of the bear are very important. The bear needs to have floppy arms. There are many bears whose arms are a natural extension of their bodies. This is not good. The arms should be separate in such a way that if you sit the bear down, you should be able to lift the arms without lifting the rest of the bear. The reason for this is that the bear will more easily mold to the contours of the body, and will feel much more comfortable. This will make it easier to sleep with your bear in your arms.

7) Consider the legs and feet of the bear. The legs do not need to be as floppy as the arms, but they need to be at least somewhat movable. Also, there should be a small space between the legs of the bear. Many bears do not have this. The reason you need this feature is because sometimes you do not feel like holding the whole bear, and a space allows you to use your arms to snuggle just the legs, which can be like having a separate, smaller bear. Your bear should also have feet. Preferably big feet. The bigger the feet are, the better your bear will be.

8) What color is your bear? Any color on a bear is okay with the exception of white. You should not have a white bear or a polar bear. It is too easy for dirt to show up on a white bear. And who wants to hold a dirty bear? A light brown or tan color is very popular, and may be the best overall color for a bear.

9) Look at the fur on the bear. The bear should have fur. There are many bears that are made with a material that is not fuzzy. But too much fur can also be a problem. Be sure you have a bear with short fur. Long enough so your hands know that the fur is there, but short enough that it does not get in the way. The fur on the ears is a special concern. For optimal use, the fur on the front of the ears should be just a bit shorter than the fur on the rest of the bear. The fur on the back of the ears may be the same size.

10) Finally; you should make very sure that you have a washable bear. Many bears may not be washed, or may be only dry cleaned. Find a bear that may be machine washed and tumble dried.

Clothes on a bear can be a problem. If the bear is for decoration, clothes on the bear are fine. But if you sleep regularly with a bear, all clothes and ribbons should be removed for best performance of said bear.

All tags on the bear should be removed prior to use. Most people remove all but the tag on the bottom with washing instructions. For best results, this tag, too, should be removed, leaving nothing but the bear itself to enjoy.

I also recommend not going back to the bear you used as a child. If you still have this bear (as many people do), that bear has already served a beautiful purpose, and should now be allowed to rest. I would suggest that you start over with a new bear.

At first, sleeping with a bear may seem a little out of place, but you will soon get used to it to the point where you become very comfortable, or perhaps even bearly addicted. This is nothing to worry about.

I believe that taking into account the checklist above when acquiring a bear will yield the best product. Despite the fact that it is not thought of as "macho" to sleep with a bear, it can still produce very good results, and should be considered not only for and by children, but also by adult males and females alike.

INTRODUCTION TO POETRY

I have often thought that poetry existed for just one purpose; to show us how we see ourselves. To give ourselves a spiritual mirror with which to gaze at the wonder of humanity. Poetry can also be used as a window. Looking through the glass of words, you see into the private world of the writer.

There are but four things needed to create quality poetry. Pencil, paper, emotion, and inspiration. Armed with these tools of construction, we build our windows and mirrors to share with the rest of the world, or to share privately with that special someone.

But poetry has also had another meaning for me. When I first started writing, the purpose of that writing was one of "Sanity Maintenance." That's all it was. I didn't know, when I started, if I had any talent or ability to write. I only knew that somewhere, there had to be an escape from the unspeakable horrors I was witness to (and sometimes a part of) on a daily basis while in the institution. I also knew, as I had always known, that man's endless quest for immortality had already been achieved. The written word has been, and will always be, the one true answer to immortality.

Shakespeare, Poe, Franklin and Jefferson, all of these great men still live today. Milne, Anthony, Nash, and even Gene Roddenberry, while a little more contemporary, will also live forever. The same can be said of everyone who has ever written anything. As long as somewhere, there lies something that you have written, you remain alive.

Poetry is a unique form of writing. It can do something no other form of writing can do. It can express complex emotion in a way that is undeniable and clearly understood. There simply is no better way to grasp the true measure of a man than by reading his poetry. It is therefore to this end that I introduce the essays and poems on the following pages. Wherever possible, I have tried to put the date they were written:

Dreamchild

I know that you are lonely,
and I know that your life is dull.
I know that your past has given you fears
and your back is tight against the wall.
I can tell by your looks you are hurting,
I can see by your eyes that you're stoned.
And it's hard when you don't want to be with people
and you also don't want to be alone.
Though it's hard to go on living
when your life has been untrue,
you can do it, Dreamchild,
I have faith in you.

You say that people don't love anymore
and you tell me that people don't care.
But I've seen you have a few close friends
who always seem to be there.
Yet to you, somehow, they're far away,
and as you wonder if they are real,
all of your questions are answered
because friends always know how you feel.
And time becomes your enemy
at the dawn of another day.
Just hang on, Dreamchild,
you will be okay.

I've seen you in times of trouble,
and I've seen you run away.
I've seen you hiding and shaking inside,
afraid to face the next day.
I've seen you in times of happiness,
times when you were shining strong.
And I've seen you in times of challenges,
times when you could do no wrong.
I've noticed you helping others,
and I've seen you follow the call.
So don't give in, Dreamchild,
I don't want to see you fall.

94

Next time you feel like running scared,
tilt your head to the stars.
Ask them where you are going.
Ask them who you really are.
Then slow down, relax for a while,
and wait for their reply.
I know what they'll say, I created them
around the time I created the sky.
So remember me in the morning.
And even though the world has died,
don't be afraid, Dreamchild,
I am by your side.

[05/22/86] Ever have one of those bad days at work? It was after one of those days that I wrote this. I had no idea this would go on to win an award. I wrote it to remind me that there are forces greater than what we can comprehend out there, and to remind me that one bad day does not mean the end of the world. I consider this poem to be one of my better pieces of writing.

Dreams: Run Of The Raven

I woke up this morning and I got out of bed.
Walked up to the mirror, took a look inside my head.
I didn't see me there, I saw someone else instead.
I started to cry and I went back to bed.

So now I am lost in the world of my dreams.
Everything's different, at least that's how it seems.
Emperors, empresses, nightmares and screams,
lovers broken up, lovers redeemed.

Egypt, with its pyramids frozen in ice,
floated over oceans, through the valleys of kings.
The beautiful balloons made me look twice
as I sat down to listen to the song the raven sings.

I saw her coming toward me, she was moving real slow.
As red as the blood that helps her to grow.
Closer and closer came this immortal from the sky.
She landed in my hand, she fell asleep, and she died.

Then I was walking through a city renamed "Stone."
I saw hills and valleys and animals out grown.
They were fighting the plants who wanted to be alone.
The raven disappeared, I heard the weeping willow moan.

And I walked along looking up to the sky.
I was asking myself questions, wondering "why."
Then I woke up, and it was easy to see
that people live and die, love and hate over dreams.

Note: This poem took me six months to write. I was in the day care center in the hospital at the time. And even when I had finished it, I had this sense that it was incomplete. Who was this raven? Was there more of a message the raven was trying to convey? If so, what exactly was said message? These questions literally nagged me for years. Then, four years after I wrote this poem, I wrote the poem on the following page. I knew there were answers to these questions, and I knew that I would like what those answers were. The problem simply turned out to be that it took me four years of searching to find them.

Dreams II: Return Of The Raven

People live and die, love and hate over dreams.
The thought crossed my mind as I got out of bed.
People live die, love and hate over dreams.
I pondered that dream and the message it said.

Through the window, I could see all the snow falling down.
Floating serene before touching the ground.
And I walked outside, asking, "How can this be?"
The raven in my dream had appeared in the tree.

I saw her thoughts clearly in my mind's eye.
She said, "I'm sorry to scare you, my name is Shaddai.
Through pyramids, balloons, and your dreams I flew
because there are words that I must say to you."

She said, "People want peace, and they want it worldwide.
Unwilling to work, they won't reach this goal.
Still, they can have peace that they cannot hide
if they turn the search inward, to the depths of their souls."

She said, "Go and sing. You have nothing to fear.
The touch of a song can humble the proud."
She then gave me songs for others to hear,
she said to sing out, to sing long, and sing loud.

She spoke again softly, and then said good bye.
And spreading her wings, she flew back to the sky.
I just had to smile as she faded from view.
Not all dreams are crazy, and some dreams come true.

Love Is There

The sounds of silence pervade my being
as I enter this world.
This world where I hear no one
and no one hears me.
You talk to me.
What do you say?
I gaze quizzically
into your eyes.
I know you are trying
to reach me.
Tears of frustration
run down my cheeks.

I turn away.

You may not
see me like this.
It wasn't always this way,
once I could hear.
My ears would sing
with the melody
of voices.
But that song
is over now.

I turn back to you.

You softly, gently,
put your arms around me.
Your eyes glow with warmth.
Your skin is soft.
You put your hand in mine.
All at once,
I understand.
All at once,
I know love is there.
For I have heard you smile.

Note: I wrote this poem during my mental health classes in college. We were assigned to visit a school for the deaf. I wrote this poem and tacked it onto the end of my report.

Later In The Morning

Early in the morning,
I watched you walk away
where sunshine kisses butterflies
and dancing flowers play.
The pain then came into your heart
and served just to remind you
that you're lost inside a hungry world
that wants so bad to find you.

The silver crown sits on your head;
what can they give you now?
All those sex-starved gentlemen
seem vague to you somehow.
You stare into those hungry eyes.
The thoughts, you cannot miss.
You soon see through their false disguise,
and you want more than this.

But what we had was different,
you can ask what it was of.
I turn this question back to you;
what is sex without the love?
Search hard for the answers,
I will wait here patiently.
Then later in the morning,
you'll come back to me.

Later in the morning,
you shall know my love is real.
That I care less about how you look,
and more about how you feel.
For I, too, have been hurt before,
I understand your pain.
I'll hold you while you cry out loud
so you'll feel good again.

Later in the morning,
you will come to understand
that I've been through that hell before,
you'll hold my shaking hand.
Later in the morning,
you will realize it is true
that you need this love from me
like I need love from you.

But that's later in the morning,
for now it is still dark.
So I'll wait for you to come around
and for the fire to start.
And when it's burning brightly
and there is light enough to see,
later in the morning,
you'll come home to me.

Note: I wrote this for Melanie just before we started dating. She was telling me there were other guys interested in her, and I certainly didn't want that. So I decided to write her a poem, thinking it was not likely that any of the other guys would do it. Later in the morning, she came home to me. At least for a little while.

Lovely Tonight

Lost in the wild wood,
alone in the world.
Somehow you found me,
you beautiful girl.
Piper, he led you
straight to my heart.
Now we're together,
we never will part.

Gentle breeze plays a song
lovely tonight.
Under the stars,
I am holding you tight.
Quiet cool evening,
soon will it fade.
Come lie with me, girl,
I love you.

I see the light now shine
soft in your eyes,
your love for me
slowly on the rise.
Tapestry caught us,
in Love we abide.
Now we're together,
I'm strong by your side.

Sing, sing a song
lovely tonight.
Under the stars,
I am holding you tight.
Love I have for you
never will fade.
Come lie with me, girl,
I love you.

> *Note: These are the lyrics to a song I wrote many years ago.
> And it was partly because of this song that Melanie accepted
> my proposal.*

More Than A Princess

Flowers on the hillside bloom in rhyme
and the crickets want to talk to you.
Somehow, it all seems so well timed
as they all sing a song or two.
And the flowers have innocence in their eyes,
and their song is worth more than a gem.
And you are more than a princess, girl,
so you know you blend right in with them.

How do the flowers know who you are?
How do they know what to say?
They were born with majestic qualities,
and they've kept them to this very day.
I love to walk with you hand in hand
and see your lovely light shine through,
and I know you are more than a princess, girl,
every time I put my arms around you.

I can't understand it,
but I'm glad to see
all of the love
that you have put into me.

The flowers and I, we have tales to tell
about the glory days back when
all of the times we were put through hell,
and you got us on our feet again.
So keep your head to the eastern sky.
The time is coming, we all will go far.
And you are much more than a princess, girl,
and I love you the way that you are.

My Grandma's Store

You're looking for a way
to fulfill your every need.
Or maybe you want a little love
with a trade in on your greed.
Maybe you want happiness,
or maybe you want wealth.
Or maybe you wish you could have
a little better health.

Maybe you want sunshine
on this cloudy day.
Or maybe you'd like Friendship
to come on out and play.
I can take you to a place
that has all this and more.
Just follow me on down the road
to my Grandma's store.

If the clouds are overcast
and no light can shine through,
or if you're feeling like the sky,
feeling rather blue,
or if you're looking for a way to fix
your spirit that's all tore,
you'll find a spirit sewing kit
at my Grandma's store.

If you think you have searched everywhere,
every cranny and nook
to find the key that unlocks your heart,
you've got one more place to look.
Follow highway sixty-one,
there is no blood or war.
And the key comes with a guarantee
at my Grandma's store.

Maybe you want true love
to help you with your life.
The perfect sort of husband,
or the lovely kind of wife.
What you want will greet you
right inside the door
if you take the Northern entrance
to my Grandma's store.

Maybe you want someone there
to help you light the way.
To lift you up, calm you down,
or resurrect you one fine day.
You're looking for a Savior
who knows what else you're looking for,
and He's there in aisle seven,
at my Grandma's store.

Grandma's have that very special
kind of slight of hand.
But her place is hard to get to,
it's in a paradise land.
It's packed with special objects
from the ceiling to the floor,
and they all come free with batteries
at my Grandma's store.

Note: Wouldn't it be nice if life was really like this?

Silent Screams

A cold and dark and rainy night,
she crawls into her bed.
She's not quite sure what kind of thoughts
are going through her head.
She listens as the gentle rain
falls softly to the ground,
and she wishes it would rain inside
instead of pouring down.

She's walked up to many people,
not knowing what to say.
They missed the cries within in her eyes
and she was pushed away.
All she wanted was someone there
to talk to and to hold.
But they told her she was crazy.
She believed as she was told.

She knew a time, not long ago,
when she used to smile.
But the world is now against her,
and it has been for a while.
She thinks of life she used to know
every now and then,
but she's been hurt too many times
to ever talk again.

Deep inside, she knows it's just
another normal night.
They throw her in the padded cell
and lock the door up tight.
There she lives among the ruins
of old and faded dreams,
where no one cares enough to hear
one girl's silent screams.

Note: This has autism written all over it. I didn't realize that until just now. I wrote it back in 1988. I wrote it while I was working at Medicare. They put me in a cubby and I took advantage of the privacy to write this. Didn't get much work done that day.

Prayer Poem

I look around this world
and see the pain in people's eyes.
I put my arms around my friends
and feel love on the rise.
But now it's all a mystery.
You seem so far away.
Help me make it through the night
to live just one more day.

And tell me where to find your love
that's lost down deep inside.
Give me the key to your heart,
and put me on your side.
Help me to think there's been some good
in all the deeds I've done,
and help me to sleep peacefully
and to wake up with the sun.

I do not know what I have done
to deserve to live some more.
And I don't know why you put us here,
or what our lives are for.
I remember waiting in the night
for you to arrive.
I should have died so long ago,
but you've kept me alive.

Please help me now to understand
my thoughts all my tears.
And I have always wanted to know
why I've lived these extra years.
I hear somebody calling me.
The voice comes afar.
I hear somebody calling you
who wonders where you are.

I don't know how to capture life
when death is still so near.
So keep me from the drawer of knives

that lies right over here.
And turn me from the bottles
and the poison down within.
Turn me instead to your smile,
let me feel your warmth again.

Help my eyes to find the good
when there's no good in sight,
and help my heart to find your flame
on those lonely nights.
Let me know you love me
no matter what I do,
and that even if I die tonight,
I'll find my way to you.

Note: This was inspired by two things. Amy Grant's "My Father's Eyes," and the outlined epitaph poetry series I did long ago. I wrote them, as I wrote this, to keep myself occupied so I could get the suicidal tendencies out of my head. Seems to have worked. I am still here.

Lavender Field/Midnight Moon Ride

The midnight moon struck violently
and cast its burgundy glow
into my eyes, which silently
took me away to the show.

Surrounded by the lavender field,
a unicorn flew down and said,
"If you mount on my back with the sword and the shield,
I'll take you to the dead."

"How can this be, Mr. Unicorn?"
I said to him, quite surprised.
He said, "Now don't look so forlorn,
their secrets will be undisguised."

I said, "Where are the sword and shield?
I don't see them on your back."
"My boy," he said, "Look to the lavender field."
Then he flew off on wings of black.

I walked around, till I tripped on the hole,
and I noticed there were two others here.
As I ran down the hill, I stepped on the scroll,
Though its meaning, to me, was unclear.

I walked all over that lavender field.
I was thinking, What does it mean?
I cannot find the sword and the shield,
they are nowhere to be seen.

That's when the big stone caught my eye.
I stood for a moment to stare.
Then I thought, what can it hurt to try
looking around over there?

And so my feet started to pave
across the lavender field.
Around the stone, into the cave,
where I found the sword and the shield.

The scroll's meaning was clear to me now
as I stepped out into the sun.
The unicorn said, "I don't know how
you got to be such a fortunate one."

And I laughed as I mounted onto his back
along with the sword and the shield.
We then flew away on his wings of black,
away from the lavender field.

Softly With The Rain

She sits in the dark.
She's waiting for someone to call her own.
Her memories flicker back
to the lonely days gone by.
She stands up to depart,
and she wonders what the evening has shown.
Tears fall from her eyes
as she walks the streets alone.

He talks to the night.
He's waiting for someone to call his own.
His memories flicker back
to the lonely days gone by.
He knows it isn't right,
and he wonders what the evening has shown.
He doesn't know where he's bound
as he walks the streets alone.

And people pass him by,
he's just another guy.
They are walking hand in hand
and they don't feel the pain.
People know she's there,
they all stop and stare.
They watch her as her teardrops
blend softly with the rain.

She walks toward the bridge.
She wants to end it all and she knows it's wrong,
but she can't help herself.
It's just the way she feels.
The water rushes by.
She knows she wants to fall and it's like a song
when she sees them.
She smiles at the seals.

He walks towards the bridge.
He doesn't understand at all and he knows it's wrong,
but he can't help himself.
People just don't care.

The water rushes by.
He knows he wants to fall and it's like a song
when he sees her,
and he wonders why she's there.

They pass each other by.
He's just another guy,
and she's just another girl
walking on the lane.
But as he walks away
without a word to say,
he slowly turns, hears her teardrops
blend softly with the rain.

She looks into his eyes.
She sees all of the things she wants to see.
She does not comprehend,
but still she finds a smile.
She starts to realize
she's finding a long lost ecstasy.
She does not comprehend,
but it will last her for a while.

He looks into her eyes.
He wonders how she got to feeling sad.
Then he finds a smile
that he cannot comprehend.
He starts to realize
the way he feels really shouldn't be so bad.
He puts his arms around her,
and they both smile again.

And people pass them by.
He's just another guy.
And she's just another girl,
but now they can't complain.
Everything's all right.
If you listen to the night,
you can hear them and their music
blend softly with the rain.

Heart Of Stone

You're looking for security
that's sometimes hard to find
when friends seem to forsake you
and ties don't seem to bind.
Soon you're walking by yourself,
unwanted and alone.
And a heart that once was filled with love
becomes a heart of stone.

Then nothing seems to matter
as you make your way through life,
like beating up the children
or yelling at the wife.
The pain inside you burns so deep,
and when you find that you've been thrown
into a cruel, uncaring world,
you've found your heart of stone.

But I love you, so come to me
and bring your heart of stone.
I'll build my world inside you
and you'll never be alone.
I know you're weak and heavy laden
so I'll stay with you and play.
And together, we'll watch your heart of stone
turn to a heart of clay.

I feel your hurt deep within
when you want so bad to cry.
When your marriage slowly breaks apart
and clouds form in your sky.
People that you used to love
no longer are around.
So you struggle through your loneliness,
and it starts to get you down.

You seek escape from this world,
you think it's all a scam.

That everyone's out to get you
and that no one gives a damn.
I see pain in your daughter's eye
when she turns to you to say,
"Daddy, I really care about you,
but please don't touch me that way."

I still love you, so come to me
and bring your heart of stone.
I'll be with you forever,
you'll never be alone.
I'm not like the others,
my love for you is real.
And I know your eyes will open
when your cold heart starts to heal.

Your kids don't seem to understand,
they just play with their toys
and have friends over to the house
who make a lot of noise.
Your head starts to pound,
you want to lay them in the tomb.
But instead, you just beat them up
and lock them in the room.

It was so much nicer long ago,
the kids were still so young.
But time has made them older
and a little more high strung.
You think back to the hospital
when you were crying on your knees.
Your baby girl was beautiful,
but she never got to breathe.

I still love you, so come to me
and bring your heart of stone.
I'll be right there by your side,
you'll never be alone.
I will take you to my world
with beauty you can still see.
I'll unshackle that heart of stone,
you'll finally be free.

You walk out to the mailbox
and feel the pain that kills.
No one sent you letters,
and you can't pay those bills.
Your life isn't fair to you
so you try to even the score
by tearing the bills to pieces,
but you find that just hurts more.

You seek comfort from your wife,
but she's made her last stand.
You found her lying in the grass
with a razor in her hand.
You stand by so helplessly
and watch her dark red blood
flow out of her body,
right into the mud.

I still love you, so come to me
and bring your heart of stone.
I know that you feel this way,
you'll never be alone.
Come into my parlor
and let me show you why
I can give tranquillity
and takes tears from your eye.

I understand what it's like
to hold the pain inside
when your life is on the back roads,
when your wife and children died.
I understand just what it's like
to feel so all alone,
and it hurts me that you've slowly given
yourself a heart of stone.

Nothing has been going right,
the world's no longer nice.
But the life you have is not your own,
I bought it with a price.
Why does it seem to take so long
for you to get it through?

When they nailed me to the cross,
I gave my life for you.

And I love you, so come to me,
and bring your heart of stone.
You'll be with me in paradise,
you'll never be alone.
I will take you to that place
that you've been dreaming of,
and together we'll watch your heart of stone
turn to a heart of love.

Tree House Prayer

All is quiet in this backyard,
the kids, they sleep, the stars shine bright.
Talking to you is not hard
on such a lovely, quiet night.
Yes, I know it's been a while
since last it was I talked to you.
Still somehow, it makes me smile,
for no one loves me like you do.

I can see a robin's nest.
A mother keeps her babies warm.
The tree house here is like that nest,
you hold me gently through the storm.
I won't pretend to understand
just what your love for me suggests;
I know you're there to hold the hand
of my deep unworthiness.

I know I've failed you many times
in public places all can see.
So now I come with prayer like rhyme
to ask forgiveness quietly.
I know I'll never comprehend
your love, no matter what I do.
You'll still love me to the end,
and that's the reason I love you.

I see the sunrise through the trees.
Morning seems to come too soon.
And here I am, still on my knees,
I love the time I spend with you.
The neighbors soon will be awake.
I'll climb down from euphoric height.
I'll always know it's no mistake
that I am walking in your light.

Hello, Megan

Hello, Megan,
and welcome to the world.
You turned out to be
such a beautiful girl.
It's good you're asleep,
soon you'll know everything
about secret values
that dreaming can bring.

Hang tight to your dreams
and what they cause you to see,
but never forget
just who holds the key.
The key to your life,
the key to your birth,
the key to our love,
and the key to the earth.

Search deep inside you,
His key is your goal.
Travel the uncharted
halls of your soul.
The key's in there somewhere
doing its part
to bring days to your nights
and to unlock your heart.

Watch out for the world
and the things it can do,
because if you're not careful,
they'll pulverize you.
But don't be afraid,
you can win in the end.
Just show the world love,
and just be its friend.

A new world is scary,
it will be for a while.
But it's okay to wake up,
to say hello, and to smile.
We all need more love
in this world of debris,
And I love you, Megan,
so smile for me.

NOTE: I wrote this just four hours after my niece, Megan, was born. Megan was the first girl in our family in 20 years (with one profoundly sad exception). She is a very special little girl.

FireFlyte

It seems this place has got you down
and there is just no where to go.
You want to hide away from it all
and find a place where you can grow.
I can hear your silent, subtle
tears within the night;
Let me take you away from this world.
We'll go for a ride on FireFlyte.

We'll say good-bye to all who've hurt you
and we will leave behind the chores.
We will run with the speed of the huntress cheetah,
and soar as the eagle soars.
We will climb to new heights of laughter,
forget what it means to cry,
and we will watch the colorful palette of sunset
from miles up in the sky.

FireFlyte is unlike all you've known,
it is darkness turning to light.
FireFlyte sets your emotions free,
you can watch as they soar out of sight.
FireFlyte knows your wants and your needs
almost like a mystical force.
He's the ultimate expression of freedom...

And he is one incredible horse.

Outlined Epitaph I

I've seen flowers bloom in the Springtime
But it is no longer Spring
It is dark, and my eyes are closed
My memories are dead, like my love
My arms are crossed on my lungs
Until the end
The last thing I saw was
The girl I loved
The last thing I felt was
Her tears falling
On my hand
The last thing I heard was
The sound of her crying
And that will be all that I
See, hear, feel
Until the end
My heart is depressed
Like my love
My heart is raining
Until the end
I am gone
I have walked out
I have run away
And maybe I still am running
Running from life
Running
Until the end
The end
And the
Beginning

NOTE: This poem, along with the next two, were written to keep my mind occupied so I would not go out and find a suitable way to die. The first three lines of this one, even today, serve as a code of sorts between myself and those who know me best. Basically means, "Excuse me, I am drifting into the darkness..."

Outlined Epitaph II

It's okay you say
We all feel doubt
But what's it about
I do not know
The rain fell
So hard today
Washed my faith away
Depression has me
Locked in its grip
Horrible feeling
This way
The pain makes me
Sleepy

Am I really
Going to die
Maybe I want
To die
What is it like
So quiet
So serene
Serene
And lonely
Eternity in darkness
Eternity in flames
Eternity crying
Without tears
Eternity
Eternity
Long, long time
I am lost
No direction
No way to go
Maybe death really
Is not so bad
After all
Maybe peaceful
Maybe no flames

Maybe light

No, no
Death is dark
I feel dark
Dark and depressed
So very depressed

And I know
That it is too late
For anything
I am just
One person
I will not
Be missed
Not by anyone

Good night
Cruel world
I am
F
 a
  l
   l
    i
     n
      g

       A
        s
         l
          e
           e
            p

Outlined Epitaph III

How long must I
Keep running
Seems I have been
Running forever
Running from you
Running from me
Running from
Those I love
I am tired
Of running
Yet I have
No choice
For my dreams
Always fade
And my roads
Always curve
My dreams fade
Into oblivion
And my roads curve
Down the crazy crowded
Highways only to
Shake the hands of
Naked nothingness
And I have
Met and made
Many friends
Some have left
Some remain
Some will remain
Forever
They and I have had
Many visions
Visions of light
Visions of legacy
Visions of love

And when these visions
Begin to fade

Like my dreams
I have found
They may be
Kept alive
By a song or two
But sometimes
Those songs
Allow the
Unthrilling yesteryear
To catch up with
My present

For I have no greater
Enemy than that of
My own past
And I have no greater
Weapon against my past
Than that of
Words
Words that fall from my
Crazy head down to the
Bottomless souls of the
Confused and frightened
The silent subtle shadows
Of my past seem to
Follow me and curse me
With tyranny as I
Make my way through
An idle life
But in my running
I have done my time
For my time as an outcast
has been way too long
And my times as a refugee
Have been way too many

And I realize I will
Meet my past again someday
But this time there will be
Color in my eyes
And a song in my soul
And when that day comes
I will once again

Traverse the unsanctified
Road of curves
And I will say
Hello to those
I left behind
And I will stop to gaze upon
The colorless changing hues
Only to put my arms
Around them

For it has taken
Twenty years
for Mother Wisdom
To teach me her
Most valuable lesson
And I no longer expect
What life cannot give me...

NOTE: I know that I cannot top those last seven lines, and so there will be no Outlined Epitaph IV. This is it.

Child Inside

Some people say
that life is a dream.
That it is all so surreal
and not at all what it seems.
But dreams are illusions
and sightings untrue,
and there is just no illusion
when it comes down to you.
Yet I almost believe
that this cannot be.
That something so beautiful
belongs now to me.
For you're a part of me now
and my life you will guide;
you're my son, you're my daughter,
you're my child inside.

Some people say
that life is a sin.
That we will end up as dust
where we once did begin.
They say it's already known
who will live, who will die,
and that we don't have the right
to ask anyone why.
Yet the life that you have
is just yours alone.
And you are free to make choices
all on your own.
But I am here if you need me
to hold when you cry.
I'll hold you close to my heart,
little child inside.

Some people say
that there's a Savior somewhere.
Others are searching,
asking if He is there.

The rest of them can't possibly
know how we feel.
They say that Jesus and Buddha
and the rest are not real.
Yet the mere thought of you
is all that I need
for my faith to grow strong
from just a small seed.
You're a gift sent from Heaven
where you once did abide.
And you're my little angel.
You're my child inside.

Some people say
that I won't make it through.
That there will be too much stress
for me to put up with you.
They say my mind will get cloudy
and my sad eyes will rain.
They say I'll pull out my hair
and that you'll drive me insane.
Yet I do not know
what they're thinking of,
for there is nothing stronger
than one mother's love.
So don't worry, child,
I'll just let it slide.
And I will love you forever,
little child inside.

Note: I wrote this for Gwendolyn when she announced her first pregnancy. I wrote it for one simple reason. I love her very much.

Now The Sparrows

The war was on and the sparrows were flying
high above the trees, they saw it all.
Guns were loading, grenades exploding,
one by one, the soldiers fall.
The sparrows watched, remaining silent,
hearing faint in the distance a clock's lovely chime.
They watched as the blood flowed into the mud,
and it seemed like such a big waste of time.

On the beach, the war went on.
Men fought valiantly, drenched to the bone.
Then one of the sparrows was hit by an arrow,
and found he couldn't find his way back home.
But one was watching the sparrow falling,
and he found a chance to show love that day.
Surrounded by slaughter, friends dying in the water,
he knew he had to get that bird on its way.

So the soldier knelt close to the ground
and pulled out the arrow as bullets flew by.
He then let it go, and was pleased to know
the sparrow found it's way back up to the sky.
The man slowly stood to join his army,
cringing at the sound of bullets speeding past.
Then one hit his heart and tore him apart.
He fell to the ground, and breathed his last.

While he lay there, the men kept fighting.
Too busy to notice, no one saw him die.
But the sparrow was flying, saw the man dying,
and tears slowly formed in that bird's eye.
Blood on the hillside, blood on the water.
Children lay on the sand that sparkled so red.
The sparrows saw the view, but didn't know what to do.
They just knew the world would soon be dead.

Men kept dying while others kept trying
to kill all they could, though they didn't know what for.

They just kept shooting and the air kept polluting.
Now there's nobody left to fight anymore.
Except for the chime, all is silent.
A hatred so cold did this world in.
There's bones on the ground where flies buzz around
wondering what kind of place it had been.

And now the sparrows fight the tail winds
with memories of war locked in their heads.
As they fly, tears fall from the sky.
Soon the sparrows themselves will be dead.

I Cry

I cry in the dark.
Why don't you hear me?
Are the sounds too faint for your ears?
I've missed the mark
and I just want you near me
to ease the soft pain of my tears.

I cry in the light.
Why don't you see me?
Does the sun shine too bright in your eyes?
I'm too tired to fight.
I do not want to be me,
the man who's sanity dies.

I cry all alone.
Why won't you come near me?
What have I done wrong today?
It's a soft, gentle tone,
yet you still fear me.
And you feel that you must stay away.

I cry in your arms.
Why don't you feel me?
What does it take to get through?
Where are your charms
that could magically heal me?
Please, hold me closer to you!

I cry soft in the night.
Why don't you hold me?
Where is the love you've once shown?
It seems that you might
at least have told me
that I'd spend this night all alone.

I cry in the day.
Why don't you call me?
How did I make you so mad?

I guess, today,
you don't even recall me.
And that only makes me more sad.

I cry without tears.
Why don't they feed me?
Why don't they roll down my face?
It seems, through the years,
that they never did need me.
They've already finished the race.

I cry out for love.
Am I lost in your file?
Do you feel I've committed a crime?
No help from above,
but still I could smile.
If you'd just hold me close one more time.

Note: I wrote this poem during a party I was having at my parents house. I do not recall what it was that I was upset about, but I do know I was upset. There were two girls playing on the computer in the kitchen. And while they were in the kitchen, I was in the living room crying and writing this poem. Alone.

Theirs Alone

The wind is blowing
and the dog is barking.
The snow drifts, floats slowly down
to the earth, covering it like
a child under a blanket.
A soft fire burns in the fireplace,
and the cat is sleeping.
Even through the noise of the dog,
who soon stops
to lie down beside the cat.

The dreams are theirs alone.
We may not intrude.

Note: I very clearly remember the day I wrote this. I was in the hospital. I was sitting on the top floor of a building watching the snow fall and the cars go by out in what seemed to be that all elusive "real world." I was with an adjunctive therapist who pretty much demanded that I write him a poem. (It was Tuesday, after all.) This is the result of his demand.

Armageddon Arcade

The enemies are firing at you,
and it's bound to make you sick.
They're getting closer, you better run,
but where are Jane and Dick?
And while Jack drowns his sorrows in moonshine water,
Jill thinks she's got it made.
Every cent she owns is in the token machine
in the Armageddon arcade.

The missiles are getting closer now,
the enemy is on the attack.
They are heading straight for Washington
and you had better fire back.
You hit them on target the very first time,
and in the air they stayed.
There's a new high score on Missile Command
in the Armageddon arcade.

The fighting breaks in the air,
but you are still on the ground.
The enemy is hovering above you,
and there's no one to help you around.
Do me a favor, please,
don't shoot at me.
I have a family, and I just got paid.
I'm on my way to play Space Invaders
in the Armageddon arcade.

The one you love was just captured,
they ran off without taking you.
Your friend is somewhere behind the lines,
what are you going to do?
You sneak in, you want to try to get her out.
The whole time, you are scared and afraid.
The barrel just hit Mario on Donkey Kong
in the Armageddon arcade.

The fighting breaks out again in New York

and you are frozen in fear where you stand.
Everyone is killing everyone else
every which way that they can.
You feel like you want to get stoned
and your headband just got frayed.
Defender is about to get blown out
in the Armageddon arcade.

The enemy has surrounded you now,
They want to force you to quit.
You are still wishing you could escape,
get on with life, and forget about this.
But there's all kinds of pistols staring at you
and you don't have any aid.
The hyperspace is broken on the Asteroids game
in the Armageddon arcade.

Jill is running out of tokens
and her life is beginning to fade.
Jack is so drunk, he didn't get any points
in any of the games that he played.
Jill holds high score in everything.
She's with Jack, getting stoned and laid.
They're the only ones alive, everyone else has died
in the Armageddon arcade.

Note: I also wrote this in the hospital. During the Grenada incident in the early 80's. I was watching a "Special Report" on television. The staff interrupted us to take us all out to Malibu Grand Prix to play video games. As I walked around the arcade, I began to wonder if there might be some subtle connection between the video games and war...

Missionary Heart

Turn on the TV and watch the news,
but don't think about what you see.
Hatred, destruction, political reviews,
I don't need this in my memory.
Can it be that it's actually wrong
to feel so torn apart?
Or have I been given the gift of song
along with a missionary heart?

Tell us about the homicide
committed by Uncle Sam.
Blast off into space on a permanent ride,
nobody gives a damn.
They all tell me to play my part,
to go on my way and shrug.
But there are still times when my missionary heart
wants nothing more than a hug.

I'm tired of seeing people cry
every time I walk down the street.
I'm tired of looking at gray in the sky,
the world is too cold for this heat!
The world is too cold, and so it gets burned.
We pick up the pieces, and then
every time mankind says it has learned,
we do it all over again.

Feed The Flame

Thought I saw you walking down the street last night.
It wasn't you, just the tear in my eye.
I was thinking about the reasons you weren't still around
and asking how you could have left me behind.
Now I walk through the darkness, and I face the unknown.
Today I start my life anew.
Tonight I'll cry myself to sleep lost in the loneliness zone
because I just can't get my mind off of you.

Burn, candle, burn!
Memories, feed the flame.
We all play roulette, it was our turn to lose,
and there's nobody we can blame.
It doesn't seem fair to me that most of the time,
we never get that second chance.
And while my eyes watch the sparrow fly above the skyline,
my mind is watching you dance.

Now I go on my way as I live without you,
but it gets harder with each passing day.
There was something magic locked in that smile about you,
and that's what I miss the most today.
Some would say you're gone, but you reside in my soul
throughout all of eternity.
And so I want to thank you for being yourself,
but most of all, thanks for loving me.

Note: This was written as a tribute to Lisa. Exactly one year after her death.

I've Been With Them

I've been with
the lonely ones,
the poor ones,
the hurting ones.
Their souls bleed.
Even I see
their souls bleed.
Their souls bleed and I cry.

The lonely ones are trapped
in such a darkness.
Walls all around them,
like walking in shells.
How did they build them,
these shells?
What is the way out?
There must be
a way out.

The maze runs deep
for the lonely ones.
The never ending
corridors of pain
sink into a
world of nothing.

The poor ones are trapped
in such a darkness.
Nothing all around them,
like walking in space.
How did they get there,
in space?
What is the way home?
There must be
a way home.

The space runs cold
for the poor ones.
The never ending

silent sounds
sink into a
world of nothing.
The hurting ones are trapped
in such a darkness.
Pain all around them,
like walking through fire.
Where did they find it,
this fire?
Where is the end?
There must be
an end.

The flames run hot
for the hurting ones.
The never ending
flames of heat
sink into a
world of nothing.

And their souls bleed.
The blood flows down.
Down it goes,
into the mud.
Into the mud, where it's
never seen again.
Into the mud, where it
sinks into a
world of nothing.

And I cry.
And my tears fall down.
Down they fall.
They fall on
the lonely ones,
the poor ones,
the hurting ones,
and sink into a
world of something.

Your Song, Saint Katherine

Sing your song, Saint Katherine,
sing it long, sing it loud.
Sing your song over valleys and plains
to the ears of the crowd.
For the children, they weep
where the crowd is asleep.
And they see not the danger
in the company they keep.

Sing your song, Saint Katherine,
sing the one that you wrote.
Sing your song so the people will hear
every last compassionate note.
For harmony is a ride.
Like the sand and the tide,
the notes blend well together
and they never collide.

Sing your song, Saint Katherine,
from the heights of the land.
Sing your song so the deaf and the blind
may soon understand.
For the deaf feel the song,
and the blind sing along.
And the love makes things all right
where they once were all wrong.

Sing your song, Saint Katherine,
where the rivers run wide.
Sing your song so the people will know
that you are in their side.
For the sides, they are torn
between the rich and forlorn.
And the mothers and the children
who have not yet been born.

Sing your song, Saint Katherine,
watch the butterflies dance.
Sing your song so the people can see
that they still have a chance.
To leave the unknown.
To fly away on their own.
To find the life they are searching for,
for your song sets the tone.

Sing your song, Saint Katherine,
for it burns in your soul.
Sing your song before age and decay
soon take their toll.
Before it's too late to start,
and the people drift apart
without knowing that the answers lie
within their own hearts.

Note: I wrote this for my niece, Katherine, when she was born.   Kind of a
"welcome to the world" present from me to her.

Go To Sleep, Daddy

Go to sleep, Daddy,
don't worry about me.
I'll be all right
as I hope you can see.
Get under the blankets
and lay down your head.
Mommy's gone, Daddy,
I'll put myself to bed.

Go to sleep, Daddy.
Those dishes you broke?
I picked them up for you, Daddy,
before you awoke.
I told Mommy I did it.
I hope you don't mind.
I just didn't want her
to leave us behind.

Go to sleep, Daddy.
That hole in the wall?
I told Mommy you fell,
that you had a bad fall.
That you tripped on my toys
so it's my fault again.
I took the blame for you, Daddy,
because I'm your friend.

Go to sleep, Daddy,
morning's not far away.
And you can beat me again
like you did yesterday.
I'll scream again for you, Daddy,
and put on a show.
And I love you, so Mommy
will never know.

Marriage Prayer

Lord Jesus
Guide these two on their way
To your presence
Guide them as they are joined
In your Holy name
Help them to put you above
Each other
And each other
Above all else
Help them to
Help each other to
Grow closer to you
Help them to love each other
In good times and in bad
Help them to come to know you
As you truly are
Not how others
Make you out to be
Assure them of
Your love for them
Assure them of
Their love for you
Assure them of
Their love for each other
And guide them peacefully
All the days of
Their long happy lives

Note: I wrote this the day Gwen and Michael were married. It seems as though this prayer has been answered.

Until His Son Hits Your Eyes

A new life on loan,
yet a life you now own
as the stars shine upon you a light you will keep.
In bed until tomorrow,
you just want to borrow
someone so they can come sing you to sleep
with melody so sweet and harmony so bright
as you drift away into the night.

And rock-a-bye, Baby,
until tomorrow, and maybe
you'll see your life coming so near yet so far.
Rock-a-bye, Baby,
until His Son hits your eyes,
and you realize what a beautiful person you are.

The room is now dark,
but you feel a spark
of life deep within you, His cool, Sovereign light.
Awake in your dreams,
or so it would seem
as Mommy comes in just to kiss you good night.
You reach up and touch her beautiful face,
then your mind drifts away into space.

And rock-a-bye, Baby,
until tomorrow, and maybe
your mother will rock you in the cool autumn yard.
She's a dreamer, she's a doer,
but you somehow get through her,
and teach her that life really isn't so hard.

Sleeping so silent
with a life so unviolent,
you're content living life on what little we know.
Dreaming away,
when you wake the next day,
you will teach us to love as we watch you grow.

So rock-a-bye, Baby,
until tomorrow, and maybe

you'll see your life coming
on down the way.
Rock-a-bye, Baby,
until His Son hits your eyes,
and you realize your life is beginning today.

Lost In The Dust

This is all I have of you,
it once was more than this.
These words of love that you wrote down
now serve to make you missed.
For someone else is holding you
through the night and into the day.
And thoughts of what may well have been
just will not go away.

I do not really understand,
for I was good to you.
I both held and loved you close
when love began anew.
But then, somehow, the new grew old,
It happened one dark day.
You missed the tears deep in my eyes
when you walked away.

Someone else now makes you smile.
Your love for him is deep.
In the night and all the while,
I cry myself to sleep.
We will now go our separate ways
and both do what we must.
You grow while I stay alone
with dreams lost in the dust.

This was written after Melanie and I broke up. I was cleaning out some boxes and I found one of her love letters. Then I sat down and wrote this. She has never seen it.

Love Slowly Dies

Illusions sometimes seem like love,
but we had something more.
The feelings that I had for you,
I have not known before.
Now I walk in my loneliness,
dazed from day to day.
And I realize I may never know
just why you went away.

I loved you more than life itself.
My love was greater still.
You walked away from all that love
and gave my heart a chill.
I loved more than everything
else that I might own.
But you saw fit leave me here
crying all alone.

What is love if it is not
a feeling from within?
I understand you've had it hard,
I realize where you've been.
But understand I needed you
here, right by my side.
My heart was filled with love for you,
my arms were open wide.

I loved you more than all the stars
that shine bright in the sky.
How can you just walk away
and let love slowly die?
I loved you more than all the grains
of sand now on the beach.
Your eyes, they sparkled like that sand,
but now they're out of reach.

Life was nice while you were here,
but now it's gotten hard.
Will I be afraid to love again,
will I let down the guard?

Now I go to sleep at night,
my feelings are quite bad.
I can't help but wonder what
a life we might have had.

Another poem written to soothe my broken heart.

Road Of...

I walk down
the lonely road
on a hot summer day,
with a cool wind
blowing through
my hair.
I start at the beginning,
and I see a child
playing on the swings
with some others.
But what is it
about this one child
that attracts me to him?
I do not know,
so I keep going.

The smooth road hits rocks.
And as the sharp edges
penetrate my bare feet,
I see the child again,
only he looks older.
I see him talking to others,
unsure of himself
and those around him.
I want to run up to him,
hold him, tell him
I love him,
but my feet move me further
down the road.

I have no control
over my feet
as they lead me
into rain. ·
Rain that pours
all over me
like sunshine pouring on
plants in the Spring.
But it's not sun,
it's rain.

And I turn and see that child
who ages so quickly,
running towards me.
Then, in the fog,
he disappears.

At last the rain stops
and the fog lifts.
The sun pours down upon me
as the rain did.
I come to long
steep hills in the road,
and the child appears again
at the top and bottom
of each hill,
getting older
every time I see him.

The road begins to curve
and I follow it,
seeing once again that child
who in hours has grown
from a small child
to an adolescent.
I finally come to
the end of the road,
and I see the sign.
It say's, "Life."

I wake up, finding myself
in a meadow, surrounded by
flowers, butterflies
and sunshine.
And I pick myself up off the grass,
and head towards home...

I wrote this in the institution. Kind of a biographical poem.

Listen Laodicea

Behold; I stand at the door and knock.
Don't treat me like a stranger.
If anyone should hear my voice and open the door,
I will protect them from danger.
I will come in, be with them, they with me.
Tonight and tomorrow and eternally.
Behold, I stand at the door and knock,
and I'll wait here patiently.

Your lukewarm ways, they push me aside.
I feel like you're all trying to take me for a ride.
And even though it hurts me, I don't want you to hide
from me this way.
Since the beginning of creation, I've been watching you.
I'm the Alpha and Omega, the one witness, too.
Even when you're hidden, I see everything you do.
And my love forces me to say...

That the riches you have can't compare to mine.
You're tired and you're poor, you're looking for a sign.
Open your heart, take in my love divine,
and I'll give you security.
Take in my gold, take in my clothes.
Take in my beauty, the fragrance of rose.
Take in my blessings, I could give you lots of those
if you'd just open your hearts to me.

Behold; I stand at the door and knock.
Don't treat me as a stranger.
Whosoever shall hear my voice and open the door,
them will I protect from danger.
I will come in, be with them, and they with me.
This is forever, not just to borrow.
Behold, I stand at the door and knock,
and you may not have a chance to answer tomorrow.

Based on Revelation 3:14-22, specifically classic verse 20.

Warm Nights With Sara

Sara is talking to people in the past.
She weaves her words carefully, she wants them to know.
And as she is weaving, she tells them a story
that will not be listened to long, long ago.
Sara is talking to folks in the future.
They see her eyes sparkle, but they don't know how.
And as her eyes sparkle, she tells them a story
that never was listened to long after now.

She says the living are living in danger
ignoring a truth they cannot comprehend.
But Sara knows better, she's trying to warn us
that man and creator should be brothers again.

Warm nights with Sara lie under the stars.
In Sara's arms, you forget who you are.
You see branches sway as you feel gentle breeze,
and a warm night with Sara puts your mind at ease.

Sara's a teacher, she's also a seeker
looking for truth that she'll slowly find.
Her eyes retain sparkle, and you feel the glory
as she teaches you her world, and leaves yours behind.

Her world is a carnival ride, it's a rainbow.
She wants you to be there, she wants you to see
the ways of the future, the way you are going,
to hear her story, and to set yourself free.

She fears the living are living in danger
ignoring the words and ignoring the call.
But Sara knows better, she's trying to warn us
that man and creator are friends after all.

Warm nights with Sara lie under the moon.
She tells you she loves you, not a moment too soon.
The beauty in the stars is beyond your command,
but a warm night with Sara helps you understand.

Back in your own world, back in the war zone,
you see all the hurting and feel all the pain.
It's your darkest hour but you do not worry.
There's nothing to fear, for Sara remains.

Sara will teach you, eventually reach you.
Her beautiful words cannot long be denied.
You start to listen and hear Sara's story.
In the past and the future, it's already died.

She knows the living are living in danger
running out of compassion; tomorrow, today.
Sara knows better, she's trying to warn us
that man and creator are turning away.

Warm nights with Sara lie alone in the dark.
You hold her hand while she holds your heart.
Her beautiful voice sings to the sky;
for she knows God is living, He never will die.

*I wrote this for Sara, a friend of mine. Many have told me that like Lavende
Field, the meaning of this poem becomes lost in the symbolism. Unlike
Lavender Field, I don't believe it is true in this case.*

If I Were An Archaeologist

If I were an archaeologist,
I could dig around in the dirt with special tools.
I'd uncover pottery and arrowheads and such,
then I'd gently clean them with my archaeology brush.
I would be the expert, I would be the one who knows
how it all began and how civilization rose.
And best of all I'd get to wear those neat safari clothes
if I were an archaeologist.

If I were an archaeologist,
folks would automatically think that I am very smart.
I'd speak at universities and conferences galore;
first they'd introduce me, then I would take the floor.
I'd speak to them about the great mementos I had found.
Artifacts and bones buried deep beneath the ground.
I'd gladly field some questions then from people all around,
if I were an archaeologist.

If I were an archaeologist,
maybe I could find the love that you and I once had.
I'd search for hidden treasure buried deep within your heart,
then we would be together like we never were apart.
We'd go out on safari on a bright and sunny day.
I'd be with you forever, it would never go away.
I'd hold you in my arms again and that is why I say
I'd like to be an archaeologist.

To give credit where credit is due, friend and advocate Jan Serak helped me write this poem. This is one of my favorites, maybe due to the collaboration.

For Friend Diane On Her Birthday

I don't usually write these poems,
but this time I think I can.
And all because of who it's for;
My good friend, Diane.

For there's something sweet about her.
Something deep and whole.
It has attraction all its own.
It latches to your soul.

It is something magic in her.
Is it love or something more?
She talks to you and then your heart
ascends, begins to soar.

It is something clever in her.
It always plans and schemes
while she ponders things you speak of,
and makes sense of your dreams.

It is something warming in her.
It takes away your woes.
You feel it when she touches you,
when she holds you close.

And as she's read this poem,
she's known all the while
that this one thing I speak of
is her contagious smile!

*[09/10/92] This was a birthday present for Diane D. Twachtman. Aside from the
birth poems I have written for my nieces and nephews, this is the only birthday
poem I have ever written. I don't plan to make a habit of it.*

The Future.

I have several plans of things I would like to get done in the near and distant future. Here are just some of my goals.

** Remain on the board of directors of the Autism Society and continue speaking at conferences.

** Write software for IBM geared specifically to meet the needs of facilitated communication. (And should F/C go on to eventually be proven a valid technique, maybe it will mean a little income for me.)

** Create a few more sensory devices. Look into possibility of creating socially appropriate "sensory armor" to make the overall environment more tolerable for people with autism.

** Write a book specifically for the person with autism, explaining exactly what autism is and the treatments currently available, as well as where research is going. This is a high priority goal. With all the books out there about people with autism, it is about time someone wrote a book for people with autism. There is a belief out there in society that people with autism can't read. Watch me shatter that myth.

** Obtain steady employment at autism research or information center.

** Get a group of musically savant people with autism together to do a benefit album for the ASA.

** Serve a term or two as president of the ASA. (I can only hope I come to my senses before I actually do this.)

I guess if there was one thing that I would really want to say to everyone, it would be to remember that the people with autism, regardless of all the controversies surrounding them, have intelligent thoughts and honest feelings, just like everyone else. If you tickle them, they will laugh. If you prick them, they will bleed. They are just as human and just as much of a person as you are. Let us not forget this. Let us all work to treat them with the caring, the dignity, and the respect which we would give to anyone else. Because they deserve it.

DATE DUE

IL: 6338990	AP 27 '06		
4-15-01			
	ILL		
ILL	Keene PL		WITHDRAWN
44001	4/1/02		
9/12/01	ILL		
	5786632		
ILL	5/8/02		
1890736			
11/29/01	ILL		
	7953443		
ILL	7/29/02		
3062665			
1/14/02	NO 6 '02		
	ILL		
ILL	1739525		
3479281	2/22/05		
2/14/02	AP 9 05		